FEMALE GENITAL CUTTING

TERRY TEAGUE MEYER

FOREWORD BY JEWEL MULLEN, MD, MPH, MPA
COMMISSIONER, CONNECTICUT DEPARTMENT OF PUBLIC HEALTH

ROSEN
PUBLISHING®

New York

Published in 2016 by The Rosen Publishing Group, Inc.
29 East 21st Street, New York, NY 10010

Copyright © 2016 by The Rosen Publishing Group, Inc.
Foreword © 2016 by Jewel Mullen, MD, MPH, MPA

First Edition

Library of Congress Cataloging-in-Publication Data

Meyer, Terry Teague.
Female genital cutting/Terry Teague Meyer.
     pages cm.—(Confronting violence against women)
Foreword by Jewel Mullen, MD, MPH, MPA
Includes bibliographical references and index.
ISBN 978-1-4994-6050-6 (library bound)—ISBN 978-1-4994-6051-3 (pbk.)—
ISBN 978-1-4994-6052-0 (6-pack)
1. Female circumcision—Juvenile literature. 2. Female circumcision—Social
aspects. I. Title.
GN484.M49 2016
392.1'4—dc23

                                                                    2014047676

Manufactured in the United States of America

CONTENTS

5 FOREWORD by Jewel Mullen, MD, MPH, MPA

8 INTRODUCTION

12 CHAPTER 1
Choosing a Name and Looking Back

22 CHAPTER 2
**Procedures, Health Effects, and
Complications of Female Genital Cutting**

34 CHAPTER 3
The Long, Strong Arm of Tradition

43 CHAPTER 4
**The Fight to End the Practice of
Female Genital Cutting**

58 CHAPTER 5
Surviving and Healing

77 GLOSSARY

79 FOR MORE INFORMATION

88 FOR FURTHER READING

91 BIBLIOGRAPHY

96 SOURCE NOTES

101 INDEX

Female Genital Cutting
We Have to Start Talking about It Together if We Want to Stop It

Jewel Mullen, MD, MPH, MPA
Commissioner, Connecticut Department of Public Health

As a physician and public health leader, I know that collective action backed by public health, medical, and social science can protect peoples' health, improve their well-being, and save lives. Tobacco control, car passenger restraint, and immunization laws have reduced rates of disease, injury, and death among children and adults. However the laws were not solely responsible for those successes. Thoughtful and well-coordinated implementation of policies and strategies were required for them to be effective. Eliminating female genital cutting (FGC) requires a similar coordinated approach.

Fortunately, an essential first step to ending FGC has already been achieved through adoption of international and domestic laws that ban cutting. Such measures characterize FGC as a human rights issue, and one that lacks medical or cultural justification. Additionally, awareness about the practice and advocacy to stop it exists among humanitarians, clinicians, social scientists, scholars, and creative artists—within and outside of the communities in which cutting remains prevalent. By coordinating efforts, we can continue to increase societal knowledge about FGC and establish a deliberate way forward to end it.

What does this way forward require? First, there must be community conversations that help members differentiate elective social behaviors from imposed practices that cause discomfort, physical damage and loss of normal function, secondary disease, and sometimes death. Such discussions distinguish culture or custom from human rights offences, supporting the right of women and girls to control their bodies and their health. They reinforce that we do not abandon human rights to avoid cultural conflict. These are important topics to be undertaken in neighborhoods and school systems, as well as in medical, public health, human service, and legal communities. They should be grounded in a framework that reflects our societal obligation to protect the human rights of all people, especially vulnerable children, older adults, and the disabled.

Recruiting leadership across multiple sectors is another action essential for ending FGC. Although the health consequences of cutting have been well documented, it is not just a medical issue. Educational, child welfare, legal, and other community organizations are equally important partners. Beyond teaching clinicians about the prevalence and treatment of FGC among many populations, their instruction must emphasize prevention. Clinicians must learn patient and family interview techniques to identify those at risk, to provide education, and to refer patients and/or families to appropriate social supports to ensure that girls' rights are not violated. Collaborators, including those from communities in which FGC has been practiced, should help design and deliver the training. Collectively, they should identify strategies and best practices that uphold child welfare policies. They also must avoid stigmatizing families or accelerating legal penalties. Similar training and community supports must be available to teachers and other school personnel. Committed school administrators, supported by policy makers at the state and local level, can make those resources available.

Finally, discussing the imperative to end FGC as a human rights rather than cultural issue requires that we continuously strengthen our understanding of and respect for diverse communities across our nation and the world. We must remain aware of our own assumptions and beliefs in our outreach to others. Fundamentally, we must also be prepared to undertake frank conversations about females' genitalia in order to advance strategies that protect their physical, emotional, and reproductive health. Our ability to conduct those frank conversations will convey to girls, women, families, and communities that we care about them, we respect them, and that we will join hands with them to ensure their rights are upheld.

INTRODUCTION

In the short film *Female Genital Mutilation: A Change Has Begun*, five women living in the United Kingdom describe the ordeals they suffered. Each woman experienced female genital cutting as a child. Their countries of origin vary, as do their ages at the time of being cut. One was cut at the age of seven. Another woman recalls being sixteen at the time, the oldest in a group that included a two-year-old (who later died from complications relating to the procedure). Now, as adults, these women can't forget the experience, and each tells much the same story. What follows is a collection of these women's retelling of their experiences.

> There was dancing and celebration.
> It was a really big party and I felt like a princess.
> But I didn't understand what it was about and no one told me what would happen.
> Then I was taken away.
> The women held me down and cut me between the legs.
> I screamed at the pain and they gagged me.
> I struggled and someone sat on me.
> The pain was awful and I can still feel it every time I think of it.
> The pain doesn't go away. It stays with you forever.[1]

The horrible experience these women can't forget is called female genital cutting. Each one suffered from having some portion of her private, reproductive body parts cut away. Girls too young to understand

Teenage girls in Somaliland, a semiautonomous region in northern Somalia, attend an after-school club funded by UNICEF. Female genital cutting is one of the topics of discussion. In the past, genital cutting was seldom discussed in the cultures where it was practiced.

sexuality or the workings of their bodies are surgically transformed for life, often by people with no medical training. Important healthy body parts are cut away. Many young girls are then crudely stitched back together. As the personal accounts in the film indicate, these procedures affect women both physically and emotionally for life.

Today the women whose voices are heard in this short film are working through the organization FORWARD (Foundation for Women's Health, Research and Development) to educate the public about the damage caused by female genital cutting. Their voices can be heard on FORWARD's website. Many such organizations are working to raise awareness about female genital cutting and bring an end to the practice. Victims of female genital cutting are speaking out and learning about ways to heal physically and emotionally. A change has begun, but the struggle to end the ancient practice of female genital cutting has a long way to go.

Female genital cutting is an ancient tradition still widely practiced around the globe. According to a World Health Organization (WHO) fact sheet updated in 2014, more than 125 million girls and women alive today have been subjected to some form of genital cutting or mutilation in the 29 countries in Africa and the Middle East where the practice is most common.[2] But genital cutting doesn't happen only in faraway countries. According to the most recent available figures, from preliminary data reported by the Population Reference Bureau in February 2015, 507,000 women and girls in the United States have suffered from such procedures or are at future risk.[3] Evidence of cutting taking place within the United States is suspected, but hard to confirm. The practice was outlawed in the United States in 1996. The majority of those at risk would be taken abroad for such procedures.

Female genital cutting has no medical benefits. Instead, the practice can lead to horrible health consequences—both physical and mental.

Yet a 2013 report by the United Nations Children's Fund (UNICEF) projected that an additional thirty million girls could be affected in the Middle East and Africa during the next decade.[4] The number of girls at risk in the United States has increased by 35 percent between the years 1990 and 2000.[5] Why then does the practice continue?

Tradition and a sense of cultural heritage are strong forces that keep the practice of female genital cutting alive. People around the world grow up with a native language and customs that shape their thinking. The foods they eat, the holidays they celebrate, and the ways in which friends and family members relate to one another are examples of cultural differences that affect behavior. People assume that their own upbringing is normal, and they pass familiar customs along to their children. Customs relating to courtship, marriage, and sexual relations are important in forming the social fabric of any culture. The strong influence of tradition enables practices like female genital cutting to continue into the twenty-first century.

Female genital cutting has a long history. The practice continues in spite of international efforts to stamp it out. But progress is being made around the world through changes in laws and attitudes. This resource will provide an overview of female genital cutting—its many forms and the wide-ranging health problems it poses for women.

The long history of female genital cutting has led to the present, when efforts are being made to eliminate the practice. Support is growing to protect those at risk for cutting. Women suffering from the mental and physical effects are breaking their silence and learning how to heal. Their voices must be heard so that others will join to help bring an end to this form of violence against women. By learning about this painful means of oppressing women, people can join in working to eliminate the practice of female genital cutting. Now is the time to act.

CHAPTER 1

Choosing a Name and Looking Back

Those who support the practice of female genital cutting often use the term "female circumcision" because it suggests a procedure that is much the same as male circumcision. However, the two practices are widely different in purpose and outcome. As the

Before procedure	After procedure

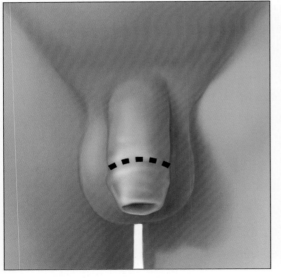 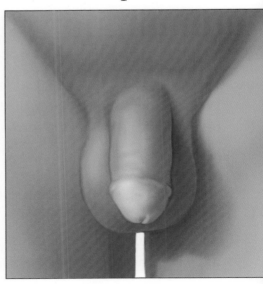

Foreskin is cut along dashed line

Foreskin is removed

Before and after illustrations of male circumcision show that the male genitals are minimally changed by the procedure. Unlike female genital cutting, removal of the foreskin does not affect the male's ability to reproduce or urinate.

human rights organization Equality Now points out, female genital cutting is a cultural tradition with the intent of subjugating women and controlling their bodies and sexuality.[1] The term "circumcise" comes from the Latin and means "to cut around." Male circumcision is very common in Western cultures. Male circumcision involves surgically removing the foreskin that partially covers the end of the penis. Male circumcision is almost always performed soon after birth. In contrast, female genital cutting describes a number of invasive and physically damaging surgical procedures that can

Clitoridectomy and Partial Excision of Labia Minora

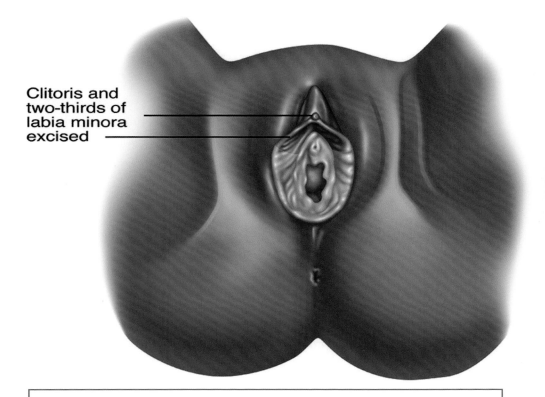

Clitoris and two-thirds of labia minora excised

Removal of the visible part of the clitoris involves cutting surrounding tissue as well. This procedure means that intercourse will likely be painful rather than pleasurable for the woman. Any such procedure puts the girl or woman at risk for many life-long medical problems.

make normal physical functions such as urination and menstruation very difficult. Male circumcision has been shown in recent years to provide some protection from the contraction of HIV and other infectious diseases. Female genital cutting, in contrast, has no medical benefits and subjects girls and women to long-term physical and emotional trauma. The extent of the damage that may be caused to a female's genitals and general health makes it clear that male and female circumcisions are not really similar. Some people who recognized the risk in the practice began using the term "genital mutilation" in the 1920s, and this term became more common in the 1970s. In the early 1990s, both the WHO and the Inter-African Committee on Tribal Practices Affecting the Health of Women and Children began calling this range of procedures female genital mutilation.[2] Many health care providers prefer to use the term "female genital cutting" rather than "female genital mutilation" because of how a woman defines herself in the wake of such a physically and psychologically traumatic assault. Psychologists are in agreement that the way a person defines herself is impactful in how she lives in the world. The term "female genital cutting" (FGC) will be used throughout this resource.

A Long History of Ways to Control Women

Writings in history, literature, and folklore from around the world reflect several views of females that explain the many forms of traditions of controlling women and their bodies. Women are seen as weak, both in body and mind. From this attitude, it follows that women need men to protect them and make decisions for them. Women are also seen as lustful temptresses who have difficulty controlling their sexual urges. Furthermore, women are regarded

FEMALE GENITAL CUTTING:
ANCIENT HISTORY TO THE PRESENT

The origins of female genital cutting are unknown. The earliest mention of the practice is found in the works of the Greek historian Herodotus in the fifth century BCE. He noted that Egyptians practiced circumcision on both males and females. Another Greek, Strabo, also wrote about the practice after a visit to Egypt in 25 BCE.[3] The practice became linked to slavery in Egypt, where cut female slaves brought a higher price.

During the long history of Egypt, the practice of female genital cutting became the norm for women of all classes. Mona Eltahawy, an Egyptian national, stated in a 2014 *New York Times* article that Egyptian government figures put the rate of female genital cutting at 91 percent of the female population between the ages of fifteen and forty-nine.[4] Over time, the practice spread across Africa and the Middle East; it is most common in the western, eastern, and northeastern regions of Africa and the Middle East. According to the WHO, more than 125 million girls and women alive today have been cut in the 29 countries where the practice is most common.[5] But immigration has spread the practice around the world.

as the property and playthings of men, as reflected in the idea of a harem or the modern "trophy wife." Such views have made women and girls subject to many types of control across the centuries and in many different cultures.

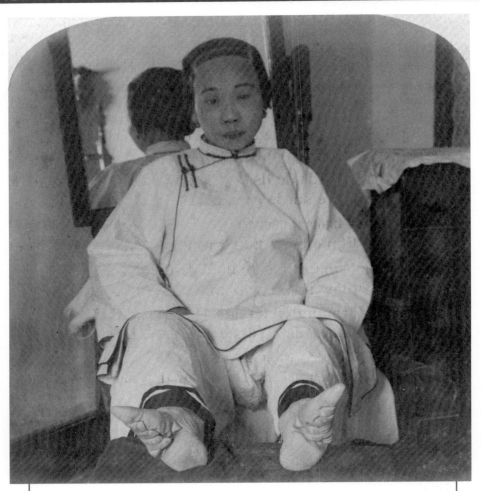

The practice of foot binding in China made it impossible for noble women to walk on their own. Yet the culture at the time valued bound feet over normal ones. Even after the practice was banned, it continued into the early twentieth century.

Whether to protect women or to protect men from women's charms, whether to hide women or make them more attractive, females have undergone many types of abuse over the ages. In addition, the common system in which property and goods pass from father to son made the issue of paternity very important in many societies. There is never any doubt as to who gave birth to a child, but the identity of a child's father is not so certain. Men have devised a number of ways to control their wives and to ensure they do not end up caring for another man's child. Female genital cutting is an extreme form of such control. The young girl who has been cut will associate her genitals with pain rather than pleasure and be less likely to engage in sexual contact or exploration. Without the sensitive clitoris, a young wife is unlikely to enjoy sexual relations, even with her husband. Even worse, infibulation (see pp. 25–29) creates a physical barrier to sexual intercourse. All forms of genital cutting put the male in control of his wife or partner's sexuality.

In different places and times, societies have found many ways to police women by controlling their bodies. For ten centuries, Chinese women in the upper social classes had their feet bound

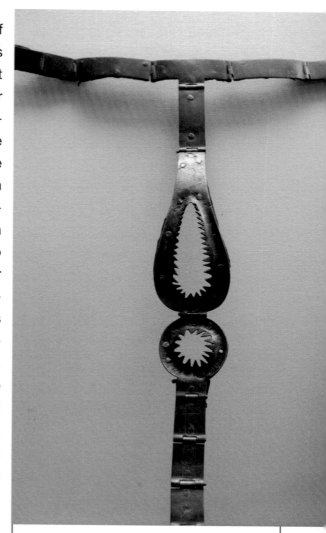

Chastity belts were once used in Europe to ensure that women could have intercourse only with their husbands. The husband literally held the key to his wife's sexual freedom.

at an early age. The binding process and the damage it did to growing girls sometimes proved fatal. A successful binding resulted in tiny, misshapen feet that made it impossible to walk. Women with bound feet were unable to go anywhere without the aid of servants. Yet bound feet were considered important in attracting a suitable husband and in distinguishing upper-class women from peasants whose "big" feet enabled them to walk and to work. The practice lasted well into the twentieth century.

During the Renaissance, European nobles policed their wives with uncomfortable chastity belts, which made sexual inter-course impossible until the device was unlocked by the husband. According to the *Encyclopedia of Dating Customs and Marriage Traditions*, chastity belts were used in Italy and Spain up until the nineteenth century. Similar devices were used on young girls in the area around the Black Sea and among the Native American Sioux.[6]

During the nineteenth century, British and American girls and women bound themselves up in corsets to meet an impossible ideal of the female body that was current in society at the time. Tightly bound corsets caused pain and fainting, but they prevented any female parts from moving and thus creating a scandal. During this same period, female genital cutting was practiced as a means to control a large number of problems identified under the name of "hysteria." The word has a broader meaning today, but at that time, the term applied to a condition diagnosed only in women. The term "hysteria" comes from the Latin word for "womb" (another name for the uterus). In many instances, doctors used clitoridectomies (cutting off the clitoris) as a treatment for a wide range of problems including insanity, epilepsy, mental retardation, and sexual practices that were considered unacceptable. Such practices included mas-turbation (sexual self-pleasuring), nymphomania (a compulsion to have sex with many partners), and lesbianism (same-sex attraction among women). The American Psychiatric Association didn't drop the term "hysteria" until the early 1950s, and "hysterical neurosis" didn't disappear from the association's *Diagnostic and Statistical Manual of Mental Disorders* until 1980.[7]

The Risk Today

Female genital cutting is not a relic of the past. The WHO estimates that as many as three million African girls are at risk for the practice each year.[8] The problem is not limited to certain countries; it is practiced by a large number of ethnic groups, particularly in Africa and the Middle East. Evidence of FGC has also been documented

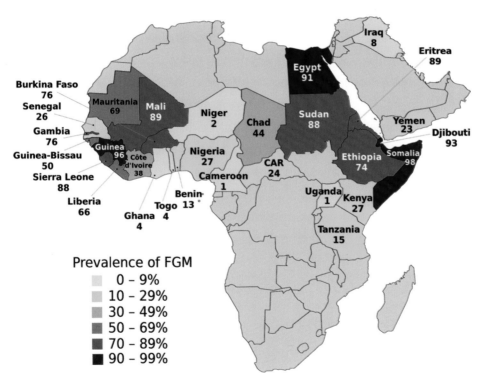

Prevalence of FGM
- 0 – 9%
- 10 – 29%
- 30 – 49%
- 50 – 69%
- 70 – 89%
- 90 – 99%

Iraq 8
Eritrea 89
Egypt 91
Burkina Faso 76
Senegal 26
Mauritania 69
Mali 89
Niger 2
Chad 44
Sudan 88
Yemen 23
Djibouti 93
Gambia 76
Guinea 96
Nigeria 27
Ethiopia 74
Somalia 98
Guinea-Bissau 50
Côte d'Ivoire 38
CAR 24
Sierra Leone 88
Cameroon 1
Uganda 1
Kenya 27
Liberia 66
Benin
Togo 13
Ghana 4
Tanzania 15

This map, prepared by UNICEF, indicates that the practice of female genital cutting is most common in a band of countries stretching across Africa. However, the prevalence of FGC varies widely from one country to another. Emigrants from these countries have carried the practice around the world.

in Indonesia, Malaysia, and India, and among the Bedouins in Israel. The practice has also been reported in South America in Colombia.[9]

Immigrants who settled in Europe and North America have brought the practice of female genital cutting along with other customs from their countries of origin. Undoubtedly, many immigrants have abandoned the practice, but others have spread the practice throughout the world. The practice of female genital cutting has spread to Scandinavia, Australia, New Zealand, Europe, the United States, and Canada. The women's rights organization Equality Now reported in 2014 that an estimated 137,000 women affected by FGC were living in England and Wales; their numbers were increasing because of immigration. In the United States, the states with the highest number of girls and women at risk for genital cutting are California, New York, New Jersey, Virginia, Maryland, Minnesota, Texas, Georgia, Washington, and Pennsylvania.[10] Women and girls from any culture where female genital cutting is practiced are at risk, particularly if their families hold fast to the customs of their country of origin. The risk is even greater for girls whose grandmothers, mothers, sisters, and other close female relatives have been cut. Sadder still, anyone who was cut as an infant or a very young girl continues to be at risk for additional procedures.

MYTHS and *FACTS*

MYTH The practice of female genital cutting is a requirement under certain religious doctrines.

FGC is a cultural tradition practiced by those of many different religions. No religion mandates female genital cutting.

MYTH Female genital cutting does not take place in North America.

The practice of female genital cutting has spread to every continent in the world, carried by immigrants who consider the tradition a part of their culture.

MYTH Genital cutting is a one-time procedure.

Certain traditions expect a female to be cut as an infant or young girl and again later as she approaches womanhood. Those who have been infibulated are cut and re-sewn numerous times.

MYTH As a long-held tradition, female genital cutting is impossible to eradicate in practicing cultures.

Anticutting activism and education efforts are showing results. Women who have been cut are choosing to leave their daughters intact. Whole villages in Africa are declaring an end to the practice.

CHAPTER 2

Procedures, Health Effects, and Complications of Female Genital Cutting

F emale genital cutting varies widely depending on the traditions of the practicing culture. In one of its fact sheets, the WHO defines female genital mutilation as "procedures that intentionally alter or cause injury to the female genital organs for non-medical reasons."[1] The same fact sheet notes that such procedures have no health benefits and are in violation of the human rights of girls and women.

What May Be Cut: An Overview of Female Genitalia

There are many popular terms for human genitals, both male and female. The term for female sex organs that seems to be gaining popularity in American culture is "vagina." But the term "vagina" does not accurately describe the organs affected by female genital cutting.

Female external genitalia

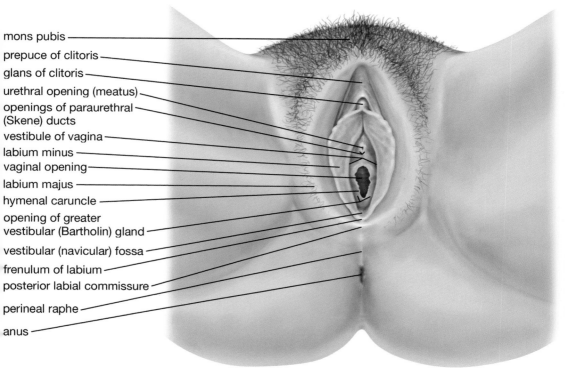

mons pubis
prepuce of clitoris
glans of clitoris
urethral opening (meatus)
openings of paraurethral (Skene) ducts
vestibule of vagina
labium minus
vaginal opening
labium majus
hymenal caruncle
opening of greater vestibular (Bartholin) gland
vestibular (navicular) fossa
frenulum of labium
posterior labial commissure
perineal raphe
anus

This illustration of external female genitals shows the genitalia to be a complex system of delicate organs. The name for all the external genitals is the vulva.

The vagina is the tubelike passageway between the outer part of the sex organs and the uterus or womb. A part of the uterus, called the cervix, extends into the interior end of the vagina. During intercourse, the male penis enters the vagina and deposits sperm. If a successful pregnancy results, the baby will eventually come out through the vagina, which is then called the birth canal. The vagina is made of elastic tissue, but it is hidden from sight.

The genitals visible on the outside of a female body are called the vulva. The vulva includes several different parts, and these are the areas at risk in female genital cutting.

Think of the vulva as a kind of doorway into the vaginal passage. This entryway is made up of a series of soft-tissue organs. Most clearly visible, particularly before puberty has caused pubic hair to grow, are the labia majora. The term comes from Latin and means "large lips." At the top of the doorway is the clitoris. This part is perhaps the most sensitive area in a woman's body. It is partially covered by a fleshy hood called the prepuce. The clitoris and prepuce are similar to the tip and foreskin of the male penis, but much smaller.

Inside the labia majora are the labia minora ("small lips"). They remain naturally closed, covering the small urethra opening (which allows urination) and the larger vaginal opening below. The vaginal opening is partially covered by the hymen, a last layer of fibrous tissue. The partial covering allows a small opening for menstrual blood or other discharge. Traditionally, the hymen is torn away during first intercourse, when it is said that a virgin is "deflowered."

The area between the vaginal opening and the anus (opening to the rectum) is called the perineum. Sometimes this area is surgically cut during childbirth to enlarge the birth canal. Tearing may also happen naturally during childbirth.

Each of these body parts has important functions for a women's health. There is no medical reason for removing any part, and doing so puts a girl or woman at medical risk.

Female Genital Cutting Procedures

The WHO classifies female genital cutting into the following four major types:

> **1.** *Clitoridectomy.* Partial or total removal of the clitoris.
> **2.** *Excision.* Partial or total removal of the clitoris and the labia minora. The labia majora may also be removed.
> **3.** *Infibulation.* Narrowing of the vaginal opening through the creation of a covering seal. The seal is created by cutting or repositioning the inner or outer labia.
> **4.** Other procedures include nonmedical harm to the genitals through pricking, cutting, scraping, and cauterizing (burning). Such procedures may be used to enlarge the vagina, to remove a hymen considered to be too thick, and to stretch the labia.[2]

A single individual might be subject to more than one type of procedure. They are seldom carried out with surgical instruments and expertise. Most often, a traditional "circumciser," often an older woman or midwife, does the cutting. Her common tools are nonsterile, imprecise instruments such as knives, razors, scissors, glass, sharpened rocks, or even the fingernails.[3]

A woman or girl's genital area is both small and very sensitive. Even the most expert practitioner damages the female body by cutting. The subjects of female genital cutting range in age from infants to teenagers around age fifteen. Jaha Dukureh, an anticutting activist who lives in Atlanta, Georgia, was cut once as an infant in Gambia and again at age fifteen in New York. Occasionally adult women are victims as well.

Examples of Female Genital Cuttir

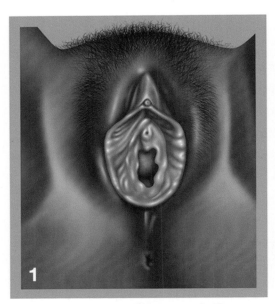

1

Vagina in its Natural State

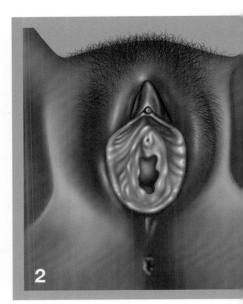

2

Clitoridectomy

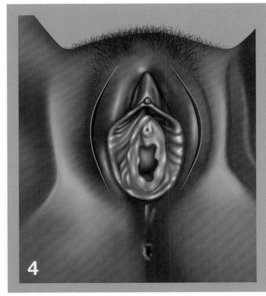

4

Total Excision

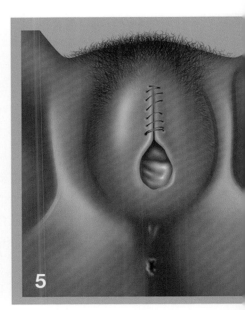

5

Partial Infibulation

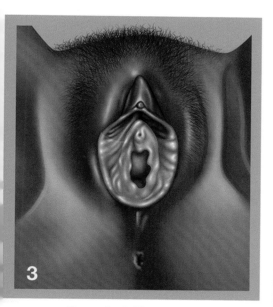

Partial Excision

The pictures at left show in purple the areas that are cut away in a clitoridectomy *(figure 2)* and the partial and total excision procedures *(figures 3 and 4)*. The appearance of the damaged tissues after such procedures would vary depending upon the techniques and instruments used. The bottom drawings, showing partial and total infibulation *(figures 5 and 6)*, make it clear how these procedures cause problems with urination, menstruation, and childbirth.

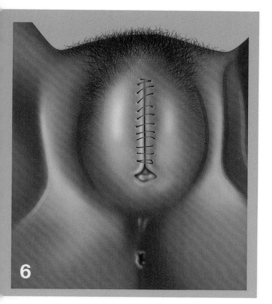

Total Infibulation

Medical Risks of Female Genital Cutting

Imagine for a moment suffering serious bodily injury while hiking or camping in a wilderness area. Without proper medical care, you would experience severe pain, shock, and loss of blood and would be at immediate risk for dangerous infections including tetanus, hepatitis, and flesh-eating disease. Female genital cutting creates immediate and lasting medical problems by removing healthy, functioning body parts. Cutting is surgery, but it is surgery performed by

BREAKING THE SEAL

Infibulation is a particularly damaging practice. In the first procedure, much of the vulva is cut away. The wounds are then closed with surgical thread, thorns, or a poultice of raw eggs, herbs, and sugar. A woman's legs may be bound together for two weeks during the "healing" process. During this time, the tissue will bond in its new configuration.

Once she is sealed in this manner, what happens when the woman marries and has children? After infibulation, a women's vulva must be opened with a knife or a man's penis for sexual intercourse. If a husband repeatedly uses a knife to open the vulva, a buildup of scar tissue often results. This scar tissue may require strong surgical scissors to reopen the vulva. The vaginal passage must also be cut open to allow for childbirth. Afterward, the vulva is infibulated again. The process must be repeated with the birth of each child.

untrained circumcisers who are using primitive and unsanitary tools. Although the circumciser tries to stop the bleeding and avoid infection, he or she is poorly equipped to avoid medical problems.

Because the female anatomy is so compact, this unnecessary surgery can cause many long-term problems. Those who have been cut often suffer from frequent infections of the bladder and urinary tract and vagina. They may be unable to have children. Those who can have children are more likely to have complications during childbirth. The narrow opening caused by infibulation leads to a high risk of stillbirths (births of dead babies). A birth canal that is blocked by scar tissue can mean long, hard labor for the mother and permanent damage in the form of fistulas. Fistulas are holes between the vaginal wall and the bladder or between the vagina and the rectum. Women who develop fistulas may suffer from frequent

A former circumciser displays the tools of her trade—a knife and herbs to heal the wounds. She cut more than a thousand girls in her native Senegal over a period of thirty years. She finally gave up the practice after people in surrounding villages decided it was dangerous.

COMPLICATIONS OF FEMALE GENITAL CUTTING

The immediate complications of FGC can include:

- severe pain
- shock
- hemorrhage (excessive bleeding)
- tetanus
- sepsis
- urine retention
- urinary infection
- open sores in genital region
- injury to nearby genital tissue
- possible transmission of hepatitis and HIV

The short-term complications can involve:

- flesh-easting disease
- infection
- endometriosis
- hepatitis

The long-term complications can include:

- recurrent bladder and urinary tract infections
- cysts
- infertility
- increased risk of childbirth complications and newborn deaths
- need for later surgeries (for example, to allow for sexual intercourse and childbirth)
- formation of obstructions and fistulas in the urinary and genital tracts

- incontinence (inability to control bladder and rectum)
- vaginal and pelvic infections
- painful periods
- painful intercourse and sexual dysfunction
- collecting of blood in the vagina or uterus
- depression
- post-traumatic stress disorder (PTSD)
- feelings of shame and betrayal

miscarriages because of urine seeping into the uterus. Victims of fistulas suffer not only physically, but also mentally. These women often smell of urine and may become outcasts in their community.

A recent movement toward the medicalization of FGC means that procedures are now taking place under sanitary conditions in hospitals or clinics and with anesthesia to numb the pain. According to the WHO, 18 percent of genital cutting today is done by medical providers, some of them in Europe and the United States. These medical providers often come from countries where FGC is commonly carried out. They operate on girls of their own cultural community at the request of parents. Although performing FGC under good medical conditions reduces the immediate risks, long-term health problems are still likely to occur. The WHO strongly condemns health care workers who perform and profit from genital cutting. In a paper proposing a "global strategy to stop health-care providers from performing female genital mutilation," the organization argues that participation by medical experts makes it more likely that the practice will continue. Genital cutting in a hospital setting makes the practice seem legitimate,[4] when it is actually a criminal act in the United States and many other countries (twenty-four countries in Africa and twelve

Egyptian schoolchildren are shown here carrying pictures of Budour Shaker, an eleven-year-old who died during a genital cutting procedure. Shaker's death led the Egyptian government to strengthen its laws against genital cutting.

industrialized countries).[5] The WHO paper particularly criticizes medical reinfibulation, the resealing of the area around the vagina, after childbirth. This procedure sets the woman up for further surgeries and increases her suffering.

Sterile conditions and anesthesia can do nothing to prevent the psychological problems associated with genital cutting. Girls and women may suffer from post-traumatic stress disorder (PTSD) and flashbacks relating to the actual event. They may also have a long-lasting sense of shame and loss. They realize that something very personal was removed without their consent.

Female genital cutting effectively takes away a women's enjoyment of sexual intercourse. Instead of pleasure, she may feel only pain. Scar tissue, infections, and the complications of cutting mentioned above can make normal marital relations a dreaded experience. The women's feeling of fear and disappointment in the bedroom may lead to depression and difficulties in her marriage. The British organization FORWARD conducted a study of the views of FGC victims now living in Bristol, England. Many of these immigrants suffered from FGC in new ways in their adopted country. They felt ashamed and afraid to seek medical help, expecting medical providers to lack understanding. Surrounded by a more sexually liberal society, they wondered about the sexual enjoyment other women experienced. One participant in the study said, "I cannot speak to my husband about my feeling because I don't even know what I am supposed to be feeling, but I saw a lot of films and saw how they felt."[6] Living among so many women who had not been cut, these immigrants longed for what had been taken from them.

CHAPTER 3

The Long, Strong Arm of Tradition

Female genital cutting serves no medical purpose and creates numerous health problems. Yet tradition in many cultures holds the practice necessary to prepare women and girls to take their place in society. The fact that female genital cutting is so widespread today shows the power of common beliefs. If everyone in a given culture believes that a girl must be cut to ready her for marriage, that belief goes unquestioned. The social pressure to conform is very powerful. In some cultures, it is possible that an intact female would be shunned by her peers and have difficulty finding a husband or a family who would welcome her as a daughter-in-law. Women working for organizations trying to end the practice tell of threats against them. Many are accused of betraying the culture of their ancestors.

Cultural Excuses for Genital Cutting

People whose cultures practice genital cutting explain that it is necessary to make a girl pure, clean, and chaste (sexually inactive). Perhaps the ancients who began the custom recognized the role of the clitoris in a woman's sexual pleasure. With the clitoris intact, a woman could experience sexual pleasure without a male partner. Her pleasure in the act of intercourse is also much greater

A young woman of the Maasai tribe in Kenya prepares to leave her home village to join her groom. Some cultures consider genital cutting necessary to prepare a girl for marriage.

because of the sensitivity of the clitoris. The clitoris also plays a role in lubricating the vagina and making intercourse more comfortable. Removing the clitoris greatly reduces a female's enjoyment of sex. According to tradition, experiencing less pleasure means a cut girl or woman is less likely to engage in sex outside of marriage.

Many harmful superstitions are associated with the clitoris. Some say it will grow long if left intact. Others believe that its touch is harmful to a man's penis. Arguments in support of cutting include false beliefs that the clitoris controls genital discharges and that the clitoris will harm a baby's head as it passes through the birth canal. Cutting is seen as somehow aiding in conceiving children and giving birth. In reality, the practice is more likely to create serious obstacles during pregnancy and childbirth.

More extreme forms of genital cutting make sexual activity painful for the woman. Clearly, infibulation, which requires a new wounding of the genital area before intercourse, puts the woman at the mercy of her husband. If having sex is painful, then the woman is even more likely to remain chaste. Sadly, even sex within marriage is very painful. And the cultures that don't allow girls to refuse cutting also don't allow a woman to refuse sex with her husband. A woman in FORWARD's Bristol study stated: "The big night or the wedding night is supposed to be the happiest night in the woman's

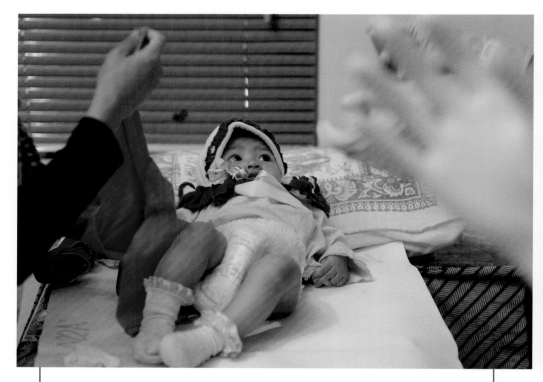

This infant in Indonesia is about to undergo genital cutting (2013). Local tradition determines the age at which a girl is cut and the extent of the procedure. In all cases, genital cutting poses a risk for the health of the female.

life. But for a woman who has had FGM it becomes the worst night of her life."[1]

Because cutting is a time-honored custom, altered female genitals may be considered more attractive in cultures where cutting is the norm. Depending on what has been done, the practice has been falsely regarded as a way to enhance male pleasure. In the countries where this belief has persisted, even women have been known to propagate this falsehood.[2]

In many cultures, a girl's virginity is closely associated with her family's honor. The male head of the family is seen as having control over that honor rather than the girl or woman herself. Girls who wish to marry someone of their own choosing may be killed—particularly if the man is someone outside the family's ethnic group. Genital cutting is a preemptive way to assure that a girl remains chaste and under male control. Those in power have every reason to continue traditions that keep them in positions of authority. The circumciser who performs the actual cutting also wants to protect his or her source of income and position of honor in the community.

The ritual of genital cutting could not go on without the support of women. Victims of cutting recall being held down by local women during the ordeal. Mothers and grandmothers offer up the next generation to this practice because they consider it a normal rite of passage for women. They may also feel pressure from those around them and concern that their daughters will not be able to find husbands. Grandmothers sometimes pressure reluctant parents, arguing that uncut girls will be shamed because society will see them as unclean or impure.

A 2014 *New York Times* article reported that female genital cutting may be on the rise in the United States because of increased immigration.[5] The actual procedures seldom take place in the United States, as the practice was banned by federal law in 1996.

RITES OF PASSAGE

A rite of passage is any ritual or ceremony that marks a transition from one stage of life to another. For example, a graduation celebrates the completion of education, and an induction ceremony may mark entrance into the military. Puberty is a natural physical transition from childhood into adulthood, and many cultures mark this period in a young person's life in a special way. Religious rites of passage include the Jewish bar mitzvah and bat mitzvah and the Christian confirmation or first communion.

In many practicing cultures, genital cutting is performed around the time girls are nearing or undergoing puberty. Although it may occur much earlier, many cultures consider female genital cutting an important preparation for womanhood and marriage. Some consider the pain a test of the girl's ability to endure labor and childbirth. In many villages, the day of cutting involves many girls and much celebration. The 2013 documentary *Healing Magdalene* captures on film a line of young girls, their bodies decorated, waiting for the cutting to begin. Very young girls and even teens who think they understand what this rite of passage involves are shocked by the reality of the experience. As a participant in FORWARD's Bristol study expressed herself, "I think the psychological impact starts from the moment of circumcision. The girl feels shy to expose her private parts to strangers. The pain is not only from the injection, because the girl might not understand why…"[3]

Opponents of female genital cutting are making efforts to substitute bloodless rites of passage for those that

theguardi:

UN & the Guardian Campaign to End FGM

BABATUNDE
OSOTIMEHIN
EXECUTIVE DIRECTOR
UNFPA

MAGGIE O'KANE
GUARDIAN
NEWSPAPER

BAN KI-MOON
UNITED NATIONS
SECRETARY-GENERAL

HON. ANN WAIGURU
CABINET SECRETARY, MINISTRY
OF DEVOLUTION & PLANNING
KENYA

In October 2014, U.N. secretary-general Ban Ki-moon (*center*) launched a global media campaign for the purpose of helping to end the practice of female genital cutting.

injure young girls. According to a United Nations Population Fund report, the organization Sinim Mira Nassique has been a driving force in eliminating the practice of female genital cutting in Guinea-Bissau. The organization, whose name means "we think about the future," introduced an alternative initiation rite for girls that includes all the traditional elements of the ceremony with the exception of cutting. At the end of the ritual, the girls leave the scene, physically intact and accepted as pure.[4] Such rites of passage honor women and girls rather than damage them.

However, girls are still subject to "vacation cutting." Youth from immigrant families are often sent to spend time in their country of origin to connect with the people, language, and culture. Too often such trips involve genital cutting. In 2013, the transporting of a person for the purpose of genital cutting became illegal in the United States.

The United Kingdom has put specially trained child protection forces in place at international airports to watch for evidence of circumcisers entering the United Kingdom or for girls being sent out of the country to be cut.

Dr. Dhanuson Dharmasena became the first person to be prosecuted in Great Britain for allegedly having performed female genital cutting on a woman after she gave birth in 2012.

The Misunderstood Role of Religion

Some supporters argue that religious beliefs make female genital cutting necessary, but no religious scriptures call for the practice. Both Islam and Christianity support chastity outside of marriage, but nothing is said in religious writings about cutting. The practice of female genital cutting began long before the origin of either religion. Female genital cutting is a cultural tradition that affects many different religious groups. The practice is found among Muslims, Catholics, Protestants, the Beta Israel (also known as Ethiopian Jews), and animists who are not part of an organized religion. Coptic Christian sects in Egypt and Sudan continue the practice of cutting, even against opposition from the Coptic Orthodox Church. The strength of the tradition is con-fused by many with a religious requirement. A *New York Times* video on the efforts of villagers in Senegal and Gambia to end

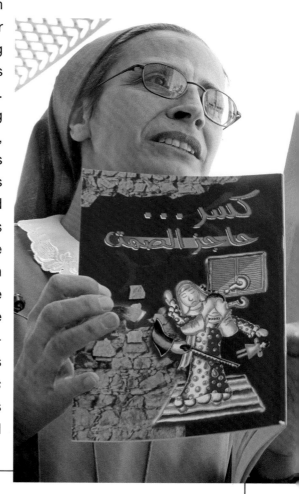

Sister Joanna, head of the Christian Coptic Center for Training and Development near Cairo, Egypt, holds a pamphlet describing the problems associated with female genital cutting. Her organization is trying to educate Egyptian Muslims and Christians about the dangers of such procedures.

the practice of female genital cutting shows an imam (a Muslim holy leader) going from village to village in an effort to end the practice. This imam uses his religious authority to educate, explaining that, in fact, female genital cutting has no basis in Islam.[6]

The imam's approach of educating people village-by-village has proved to be one of the most effective ways to bring an end to female genital cutting. Genital cutting of women and girls continues in many countries where it is banned by law, and it has spread to countries where few people are aware such practices exist. People in communities where cutting is considered a normal and necessary rite of passage into womanhood must choose for themselves to take a new path. In many cases, the push for change has come from individuals in such communities, individuals who have lost a daughter, a sister, or an infant due to complications from cutting. Inspired by their personal stories, these people are educating and changing traditions from within their communities.

CHAPTER 4

The Fight to End the Practice of Female Genital Cutting

The tradition of female genital cutting continues despite the fact that governments and nongovernmental organizations (NGOs) have been working to end the practice since the early twentieth century. The history of the struggle against female genital cutting between the 1920s and first decades of the twenty-first century shows progress toward ending the practice. This historical review also includes examples of anticutting backlash that show how firmly the practice is rooted in the cultures where it is prevalent. Reports prepared by the WHO, the United Nations Population Fund (UNFPA), and UNICEF, published between 2008 and 2013, offer a statistical overview of legal action, attitudes, and practices relating to female genital cutting in the twenty-nine countries where such practices are most common. These reports show that anticutting laws alone cannot eliminate the practice. However, by studying and analyzing surveys about the practice, U.N. agencies are learning more about the most promising strategies to reduce and finally eliminate female genital cutting.

The Continuing Struggle Against Female Genital Cutting: A Historical Overview

A brief review of the highlights in the struggle to put an end to female genital cutting shows both progress and setbacks in the struggle to eliminate the practice. What follows is largely drawn from the report "Accelerating Action Against FGM/C: Four Countries, Nine Decades," contained within the UNICEF 2013 Statistical Overview report.

In the early twentieth century, beginning in the 1920s, Christian missionaries, supported by educators, tried to abolish female genital cutting among the Kikuyu, Kenya's largest ethnic group. Many Kikuyu saw this effort as an attack on their ethnic identity and established schools where the practice was not prohibited.[1] During this same time period, the Egyptian Society of Physicians called for a ban on female genital cutting. However, Egypt would not pass such legislation until 2008.

Sudan banned infibulation in 1946,[2] but the law was unpopular and poorly enforced. During the late 1950s, a series of articles in *Hawaa*, a prominent Egyptian women's magazine, advised mothers against forcing their daughters to be cut. The Egyptian government outlawed female genital cutting in state-run hospitals. Unfortunately, the ban resulted in an increase in the medicalization of the practice elsewhere.

Ghana, Guinea, Djibouti, and the Central African Republic restricted female genital cutting during the 1960s. All but Ghana would pass additional restrictions after 2000.

During the 1970s, increased attention to issues relating to women focused on genital cutting as well. Government programs in

Djima Diallo, chief of the village of Diabougo in Senegal, poses for a photograph in 2007. That year, his village became the second in Senegal to publicly declare its decision to abandon the practice of female genital cutting. Since then, more than half of the villages in the country have also given up the practice.

Senegal promoted abandoning the practice. On the first International Women's Day (1975), popular media in Burkina Faso focused on the harmful effects of cutting. A bishop in Kenya condemned the practice as medically dangerous. He encouraged Christians in Kenya to abandon such customs.[3] France, home to immigrants from many central African countries where female genital cutting is prevalent, outlawed the practice in 1979.

International attention focused on ridding the world of female genital cutting when the issue appeared on the agenda of a WHO seminar on traditional practices affecting the health of women and

Musicians from around the world gathered in New York in 2014
to celebrate the launch of the #IMAGINE Project to celebrate
the twenty-fifth anniversary of the United Nations Convention on
the Rights of the Child. The convention, an international treaty,
includes provisions to protect children from harmful practices
such as female genital cutting.

children in 1979. That same year, UNICEF issued its first statement
on the practice. The U.N. General Assembly classified such
procedures as violations of human rights. Classifying the practice
as a human rights violation offers greater legal protection to those
at risk. In 1989, the U.N. General Assembly adopted the Convention
on the Rights of the Child (CRC), which includes protections for
children from such harmful practices.[4]

Efforts to end female genital cutting gathered momentum during
the 1990s. Laws or decrees outlawing the practice were passed in
seven practicing countries and four countries of immigration. The

Maendeleo Ya Wanawake Organization in Kenya organized the first alternative rite of passage for thirty families, which they called Circumcision Through Words. The president of Senegal, Abdou Diouf, condemned the practice of female genital cutting during a human rights conference.[5] Similar declarations followed in villages throughout the country.

In 1996, the United States made it illegal to perform female genital cutting in the United States. Canada outlawed the practice in 1997.

In 2003, the United Nations began sponsoring the annual International Day of Zero Tolerance for Female Genital Mutilation, which takes place on the sixth of February. That same year, the African Union promised to ban the practice. Since then, international organizations such as the WHO and other U.N. agencies have increased efforts to end the practice. Publications such as

On February 6, the International Day of Zero Tolerance for Female Genital Mutilation, hundreds of residents of Bamako, Mali, gather to join in a public declaration swearing off female genital cutting in 2014. It was the second such public declaration organized by Tostan in Mali.

"Eliminating Female Genital Mutilation, An Interagency Statement" and "Female Genital Mutilation/Cutting: A Statistical Overview and Exploration of the Dynamics of Change" have marked the progress made and the path toward bringing an end to the practice.[6]

In 2012, the U.N. General Assembly adopted a resolution on the elimination of female genital cutting. A press release from the U.N. News Centre on November 28, 2012, the International Day for the Elimination of Violence Against Women, reported that the United Nations Population Fund (UNFPA) had determined that eight thousand communities worldwide had abandoned the practice during the previous three years.[7]

The UNFPA also provides information on the progress of legal action against genital cutting. Since 2000, eighteen additional countries where the practice is prevalent have outlawed female genital cutting. Ten countries where immigrant populations are at risk have passed anticutting measures. A number of countries have strengthened or renewed measures passed decades earlier.[8]

Although the United States banned domestic female genital cutting in 1996, it was not until 2013 that it became illegal to transport a girl out of the United States for the purpose of subjecting her to genital cutting. The 2013 federal law aims to protect girls in America from being sent abroad to be cut. In addition, American immigration authorities are required to provide all immigrants with information about the harm caused by female genital cutting and warn about the legal consequences of performing such procedures in the United States. Penalties under federal law include fines and/or imprisonment for not more than five years. Beginning in 2014, the U.S. Department of State's annual report on human rights in other countries included a mandatory question on female genital cutting. According to the organization Equality Now, as of January 2015, twenty-three U.S. states have also passed some sort of anticutting law.

THE UNITED KINGDOM: A LEADER IN THE STRUGGLE AGAINST FEMALE GENITAL CUTTING

The United Kingdom, which is home to a large population of immigrants from countries where female genital cutting is practiced, has adopted strict anticutting measures. In the United Kingdom, it is illegal to perform such procedures on a girl or woman, regardless of her age. Her Majesty's Government published "A Statement Opposing Female Genital Mutilation," intended for young women to keep with their passports and to take abroad. This statement affirms that female genital cutting is a crime whether committed in the United Kingdom or another country. Penalties include fines and terms of up to fourteen years in prison. A London doctor and another man were first prosecuted under anti-cutting laws in 2014.[9]

An article in the *Guardian* reported on special efforts by the U.K. Border Force working at airports to keep circumcisers from coming into the United Kingdom. Specially trained child protection officers began working in the summer of 2014 at major airports to monitor for signs of travel related to female cutting, as well as trafficking and forced marriage. Since 2013, a twenty-four-hour hotline is in place to aid victims or potential victims of genital cutting.

The laws in the United Kingdom serve as a model for other Western nations, including the United States.

Turning the Tide

Because female genital cutting is deeply rooted in cultural tradition, laws and international agreements and declarations have not

Dr. Marci Bowers (*center*) consults with a Nigerian-born patient (*right*) about reconstructive genital surgery. Dr. Bowers is active in the United States in repairing the damage caused by genital cutting.

been enough to eliminate the practice. But progress is being made. The UNICEF report "Female Genital Mutilation Cutting: A Statistical Overview and Exploration of the Dynamics of Change" shows positive trends in the reduction of numbers of girls being cut. The same report shows that international organizations are learning what strategies are most effective in reducing the prevalence of cutting in practicing countries.

HEROINES IN THE STRUGGLE AGAINST FEMALE GENITAL CUTTING

Changing laws and attitudes toward the practice of female genital cutting have resulted from the efforts of many people—those in small villages as well as leaders in positions of international power. Efua Dorkenoo and Molly Melching are two women whose efforts to change minds and lives have done much to further the struggle against female genital cutting.

Efua Dorkenoo was born in Ghana but immigrated to London as a teen and became a nurse. Dorkenoo was aware of genital cutting but had not been cut. She became a crusader for ending the practice when she witnessed the terrible medical consequences of cutting on a woman giving birth. Dorkenoo worked to raise awareness of the dangers of female genital cutting on several fronts. She lobbied the British government and international organizations. She went directly to African villagers as well as to immigrants in England to educate them. She wrote articles and a book, *Cutting the Rose* (1994), on the subject. She established two foundations to promote women's health and human rights: FORWARD and Equality Now. As acting director for women's health at the WHO, she coordinated national efforts to curb female genital cutting in several African countries. Dorkenoo died of cancer in 2014. A lengthy obituary in the *New York Times* described her important work against female genital cutting and

(continued on the next page)

Women's rights activist Efua Dorkenoo (*right*) is shown with actress Meryl Streep (*center*) and Fauziya Kassindja (*left*), who escaped having the FGC procedure when she fled Togo as a seventeen-year-old. The women are at the premiere of the film *Africa Rising*. Dorkenoo was a pioneer in the campaign to end female genital cutting.

(continued from the previous page)

credited her with persuading the WHO to classify the practice as a human rights violation.

Molly Melching, an American profiled by writer Nicholas Kristof in his book *Half the Sky* (2009), moved to Senegal in the 1970s and began working in education and empowerment efforts in local communities. There she observed the importance of community acceptance and participation in making aid programs effective. Melching married a Senegalese man and focused her attention on genital cutting when her own daughter said she wanted to be cut to be like her peers. Her daughter's attitude helped Melching understand the importance of changing the attitudes of entire villages and having them make collective decisions to abandon the practice of cutting.

Melching founded the organization Tostan in 1991 to educate villagers. The name means "breakthrough" in the Wolof language of Africa. Tostan educates people about the dangers of female genital cutting by presenting the issue in a nonjudgmental way. The organization includes the topic of female genital cutting in an educational program covering a number of human rights and health issues. The Tostan model has proved to be very effective. Tostan has helped women organize joint declarations that they would abandon cutting. As reported on Tostan's website in 2014, this grassroots effort has resulted in seven thousand communities in eight African countries declaring their abandonment of female genital cutting and child/forced marriage. These declarations represent changes affecting more than three million people.[10]

Declaring female genital cutting to be a violation of human rights and a form of child abuse were important steps in raising international awareness and causing supporters of the practice to consider questioning accepted beliefs. Educating people about the catastrophic health consequences of such procedures is another important factor in bringing about change. Campaigns aimed at ending female genital cutting have sparked debate in practicing countries. The UNICEF statistical report, for example, noted that in Gambia female genital cutting was long considered secret and was not publicly discussed.[11]

ALICE WALKER: "TORTURE IS NOT CULTURE"

Alice Walker is one of the world's most celebrated and renowned living writers. Among her seven novels, four short story collections, four children's books, seven volumes of poetry, and numerous essay collections, she is perhaps best known for her Pulitzer Prize– and National Book Award–winning novel *The Color Purple* (1982).

Yet Walker is also the first novelist to confront the controversial practice of female genital cutting in a novel. In *Possessing the Secret of Joy* (1992), a tribal African woman named Tashi struggles to understand and come to terms, physically and emotionally, with the social and cultural oppression that has led her to submit to FGC. For Tashi, the result of the horrific procedure is a lifetime of pain and trauma. Some measure of healing, acceptance, and peace is experienced when she ultimately comes to possess the "secret of joy."

Having broached this subject—long shrouded in secrecy and superstition—in her novel, Walker continued to expose the oppressive and abusive practice in a nonfiction follow-up entitled *Warrior Marks: Female Genital Mutilation and the Sexual Binding of Women* (1993; cowritten with British-Indian filmmaker Pratibha Parmar, and based upon Parmar's documentary film of the same name). The book is an account of the two women's international journey to interview women victimized by FGC, those who perpetrate it, and those committed to ending the practice.

Award-winning American author Alice Walker has written both a novel and a nonfiction book about female genital cutting. She is a pioneer in raising awareness of the problem in the United States.

Both books are credited with helping to change attitudes toward FGC and building momentum toward legislative efforts worldwide to ban it and have it recognized as a violation of the human rights of girls and women. As Walker has stated, in making the case that cultural tradition does not legitimize FGC or place it beyond the reach of criminal and human rights law or moral condemnation, "Torture is not culture."

Finally, media attention from outside the country caused Gambians to begin questioning and debating the practice.

International and local groups working in the field have found that changing attitudes toward cutting typically begins with a core group who are ready to abandon the practice and seek to convince others to join them. Education and group discussion are important in spreading such new ideas.

According to UNICEF, trend data show female genital cutting becoming less common in over half the twenty-nine countries where the practice is most prevalent. An adolescent girl today is a third less likely to be cut than thirty years ago. The reduction in genital cutting is most evident in countries such as Kenya and Tanzania where the prevalence of the practice is moderately or very low. Data from Benin, Central African Republic, Iraq, Liberia, and Nigeria show that cutting has dropped by half among adolescent girls. There is also evidence of declining numbers of women and girls being cut in countries where the practice is most common.[12]

United Nations agency surveys indicate that attitudes about cutting as a cultural norm are changing. Even in countries where the practice is almost universal, support for the custom of genital cutting is declining among women and girls as well as men. An analysis of attitudes toward cutting indicates that changes in public attitudes usually come before an actual decline in the practice. UNICEF reports that nearly twelve thousand communities in fifteen countries, representing about ten million people, have renounced the practice. During 2013 alone, more than two thousand communities made such declarations.[13]

10 GREAT QUESTIONS TO ASK HEALTH CARE PROFESSIONALS

No one can underestimate the sensitivities around this most personal of subjects or the fear and reluctance associated with discussing it with someone outside the family and community. Health care professionals are, however, increasingly knowledgeable about and sensitive to this issue, its cultural context, and the laws pertaining to cutting. They are experienced and trained to offer effective help in matters relating to domestic violence generally. Questions 1-4 are valuable if you feel you are at risk of being forced to have FGC. Questions 5-10 are important if you have undergone FGC.

1. How can I resist pressure from family members to undergo genital cutting?

2. What can I do to bring about an end to the tradition of female genital cutting?

3. Will genital cutting prevent me from having normal sexual intercourse?

4. If I speak to a school counselor or social worker, how can I avoid getting in trouble with my parents or prevent the breakup of the family? How can I prevent my family from getting into legal trouble?

5. How can I find health professionals who are familiar with the problems associated with genital cutting?

6. How can I overcome my fear of medical pelvic exams?

7. What special precautions should I take to reduce my risk of infections and menstrual problems?

8. How will having been cut affect my ability to bear healthy babies?

9. Can surgery undo the effects of genital cutting?

10. Why do I feel shame for something that was done to me as a child without my consent?

CHAPTER 5

Surviving and Healing

Many people who live outside the areas where female genital cutting is a tradition do not realize such practices exist. Others only became aware of the problem when the United Nations adopted a resolution to end the practice in 2012. Sadly, millions of women and girls have personal experience with the practice and are living with physical and medical problems caused by cutting. Too many other women and girls, many of them living in North America, are at risk. Those at risk include girls and women from families coming from countries and cultures where female genital cutting is practiced. Girls and women whose female relatives have been cut are at extreme risk of being cut themselves. For those at risk or already victimized by cutting, there are now more resources available than ever before to help protect and heal them.

If You Are Being Pressured to Have Such a Procedure

Help is available to those being pressured to undergo cutting either at home or while on vacation. People in support of the practice must understand that female genital cutting is illegal in twelve industrialized nations that receive immigrants from countries where FGC is practiced, including the United States, Canada, Australia, Belgium, Cyprus, Denmark, Italy, New Zealand, Norway, Spain, Sweden, and

Somali-born activist Waris Dirie has used her celebrity as a model to raise awareness about female genital cutting. In addition to writing several memoirs, she has established a foundation to aid women who have been affected. She is shown here at the opening of the Desert Flower Centre near Berlin, Germany, the first facility in Europe to provide medical and mental services to cutting victims.

the United Kingdom. It is also illegal in eighteen African nations. So-called vacation cutting is also illegal under U.S. federal law. Organizations such as the WHO and UNICEF provide a wealth of information that can educate family and community members about the grave dangers and harmfulness of cutting. Those who consider cutting normal often don't realize that many health conditions are caused by the practice. Fistulas and certain urinary and menstrual problems that plague cut women are uncommon in those who are left intact. Those people who consider genital cutting a cultural necessity might be swayed by reading statistics showing that the practice is declining even in countries where it was once extremely prevalent. The websites for organizations such as Equality Now, Forma, and FORWARD, among others, include persuasive facts and numbers as well as personal stories telling about the lasting problems caused by cutting.

If you are at risk for being forced to undergo genital cutting, you probably feel terrified, desperate, trapped, and torn between a sense of duty and obligation, on the one hand, and a desire to break free, on the other. You are probably feeling intense pressure from within your community and even within your family to submit to what some of your elders feel is a sacred tradition. To resist and attempt to fight against the procedure and those pressuring you

A number of organizations are working in the United States and internationally to end the practice of female genital cutting and to help heal those who have been cut. Information about Forma and other such organizations are found at the end of this resource.

to undergo it is daunting, isolating, and guilt-inducing. You may be shunned by your community and family, possibly even emotionally and physically coerced, pressured, intimidated, or mistreated.

The sad truth is that, at the present time in North America, there are not a lot of places or people one can turn to for help in this situation. Even assuming one was willing to risk a potentially destabilizing and violent rift with one's family and community by contacting a social worker, child protective services agent, or law enforcement officer—a decision that could lead to criminal charges against one's family members and one's removal from the home into protective custody and foster care—not all of these representatives of public assistance are yet adequately educated in all the issues surrounding FGC or trained in how to offer those at risk effective help and protection.

Though FGC has been illegal in the U.S. since 1996, twenty-three states have laws against it, and "vacation cutting" can result in a five-year federal prison term for anyone convicted of transporting a girl or woman out of the country in order to have the procedure done, few cases are pursued by law enforcement, which, at this point in time, tends to shy away from the matter for fear of offending cultural sensitivities. Similarly, health care workers often look the other way when they are confronted with evidence of cutting, while some doctors serving communities in which FGC is practiced are pressured to perform the procedure in a medical setting. But even in a medical setting, FGC is very dangerous and has catastrophic physical and emotional repercussions. Social workers are often confronted with community members who hide what is going on, even when informed about the illegality of the practice. They also meet with at-risk girls who are too intimidated and scared of community and family pressure and potential ostracism to accept what help can be offered.

In the UK, health care professionals who suspect or learn of female genital cutting occurring in a community must share their information and concerns with law enforcement officers and/or social workers, who then investigate the situation and protect any endangered girls or women. Health care professionals and social workers are trained to give advice and information to families that is culturally sensitive and aware, while stressing the illegality of cutting and the criminal penalties. Court orders can be applied for that will prevent a girl from being taken out of the country for cutting. And any girl or woman who has already been cut can receive medical help and counseling, while any other at-risk members of her family or community are identified and protected.

North America is not as far along as the UK in effectively addressing FGC within communities, enforcing the existing laws, and offering assistance and protection to those women and girls at risk. Most activists and experts who are working hard to eradicate FGC acknowledge that, ultimately, the most effective opposition to the practice will have to come from within the community itself, a change in values and beliefs that can be advanced and reinforced by education campaigns, the active intervention of health care officials and social workers, and tougher law enforcement. But what can someone who is at risk for FGC do right now to seek help and advice?

The most important and effective first step would be to contact those individuals and organizations who are leading the fight against FGC and, most importantly, are at the forefront of efforts to protect and advocate for at-risk girls and women. They are often most directly accessible via social media. These are the people who know exactly what you are facing at home and in the community, how scared and conflicted you are feeling, and how high the stakes are for either submitting to or resisting the pressure to undergo the procedure. They also know the law, how to speak to members of your community, and how to advocate for your interests. They know the pressures you are laboring under, and they do not judge you as you struggle to find your way through this fraught situation. In some cases, they can listen, empathize, help you explore your options, offer advice, and perhaps even advocate on your behalf, or they can put you in touch with other organizations and individuals who can offer that kind of assistance.

A list of some of the leading individuals and organizations leading the fight against FGC and advocating for the rights, health, and safety of girls and women follows. Because the United Kingdom is further ahead of the U.S. in its efforts to combat FGC and protect survivors and those at risk, several UK organizations appear below:

Jaha Dukureh: Dukureh is a survivor of FGC from Gambia. She was cut when she was an infant and had a half-sister who died following the procedure. Today, Dukureh lives in Atlanta, Georgia, and is leading the effort to gather data on the prevalence of FGC in the U.S., strengthen laws and penalties, and educate communities about the dangers and destructiveness of FGC. She founded the organization Safe Hands for Girls (http://www.safehandsforgirls.org/index.html; 678-306-6717), which focuses on the effort to end FGC. Dukureh started an online petition on Change.org (https://www.change.org/p/end-fgm-now-protect-girls-from-getting-cut-and-support-victims-of-female-genital-mutilation-in-the-usa) and collected over 220,000 signatures in support of U.S. action against cutting. As a result of this petition, at a summit on FGC and child marriage in London, the Obama administration announced it would conduct a major study into FGC to establish how many women are living with the consequences of the procedure in the United States and how many girls are at risk. The administration said it would also create a preliminary working group on FGC, in order to measure its extent in the U.S. and develop concrete plans to combat and eradicate it. Inspired by the petition, in February 2015, Congressional representatives Joe Crowley

Activist Jaha Dukureh was cut as an infant in her native Gambia. She now lives in Atlanta, Georgia, and is working to spread information about the dangers of cutting. Dukureh has organized lobbying efforts to strengthen laws against taking girls outside the United States to be cut.

and Sheila Jackson-Lee introduced legislation to establish a government strategy to combat FGC, which could include an emergency hotline for girls seeking help. That would add the United States to the group of countries that have a national strategy, like England and Italy. Dukureh also created a blog entitled *Rise Up Against Female Genital Mutilation: Action and Reflection by Survivors and Advocates for Girls' and Women's Rights* (http://risingupagainstfgm.org) and uses the app WhatsApp to keep in daily contact with girls and women across the country who share concerns about female genital cutting. Dukureh can be followed on Twitter (https://twitter.com/jahaendfgm) and LinkedIn (https://www.linkedin.com/pub/jaha-dukureh/5a/839/58).

Fahma Mohamed: Mohamed, a seventeen-year-old student in Bristol, England, was awarded *Good Housekeeping*'s outstanding young campaigner of the year award in 2014 for her work to raise awareness of FGM/C in the EndFGM Guardian campaign. Her petition on Change.org appealed to the education secretary to write to all teachers in England and Wales to describe the dangers of FGC. Within three weeks, the petition had gotten more than 230,000 signatures and received the public support of Malala Yousafzai, the Pakistani girls' education advocate, and UN secretary general Ban Ki-moon. After the continuous pressure from Mohamed and others, the education secretary agreed to write to all the teachers about FGC, urging them to adopt a set of guidelines for teaching students about the warning signs and illegality of FGC and reminding them of their responsibility to protect students. At the *Good Housekeeping* awards' ceremony, Mohamed said, "This award is for all the young people of Integrate Bristol who have worked so hard over the past five years—I feel it's acknowledging the importance of eradicating FGM and protecting the rights of girls all over the world." You can follow Fahma Mohamed on Twitter (https://twitter.com/fahmaendfgm).

Forma:

http://www.formafgc.org/home.php

(877) 603-3833

The Forma website is designed as an interactive space for FGC-affected women to share their stories through art, writing, film, photography, music, or any other form of artistic expression. It is also an online community for women wishing to dialogue—either anonymously or openly—about the difficulties affecting them. Forma's mental health professionals hope to facilitate and foster conversational interventions that would validate a sense of wholeness and social acceptance for women who have been cut or are in danger of being cut.

Sanctuary for Families:

http://www.sanctuaryforfamilies.org/index.php

(212) 349 – 6009 (New York City)

(800) 799 – SAFE (National Domestic Violence Hotline)

Sanctuary for Families is New York's leading service provider and advocate for survivors of domestic violence, sex trafficking, and related forms of gender violence. Every year, Sanctuary empowers thousands of adults and children to move from fear and abuse to safety and stability, transforming lives through a comprehensive range of services including clinical, legal, shelter, children's and economic empowerment services. Through outreach and trainings, Sanctuary educates over sixteen thousand concerned community members annually, ensuring that communities are prepared to protect victims and prevent gender violence. Informed by its work with thousands of survivors, Sanctuary is a leading advocate for legislation and public policies that promote freedom from gender violence as a basic human right.

Campaign Against Female Genital Mutilation (CAGeM):

https://www.facebook.com/End.FGM

(877) 602-2436

The Campaign is committed to the global eradication of female genital mutilation (FGM). It focuses on developing and implementing educational programs to eradicate FGM and assist victims. It also fosters development of anti-FGM campaigns in practicing communities.

The AHA Foundation:

http://www.theahafoundation.org

E-mail: info@theahafoundation.org

National and state-by-state guide of resources for where to go for help: http://www.theahafoundation.org/wp-content/uploads/2015/03/aha_resource012012.pdf

The AHA Foundation is the leading organization working to end honor violence that shames, hurts, or kills thousands of women and girls in the US each year, and puts millions more at risk. AHA also works to elevate the status of women and girls globally, so they can create peace and prosperity for themselves, their communities and the world. The AHA Foundation's work is built on the belief that there is no culture, tradition, or religion that justifies violence against women and girls.

Equality Now:

http://www.equalitynow.org

Email: info@equalitynow.org

(212) 586-0906 (U.S.)

+254-20-271-9913/9832 (Africa Regional Office)

+44 (0) 20 7304 6902 (UK)

Equality Now works for the protection and promotion of the human rights of women and girls around the world. Working with grassroots women's and human rights organizations and individual activists since 1992, Equality Now documents violence and discrimination against women and mobilizes international action to support efforts to stop these abuses.

National Society for the Prevention of Cruelty to Children (NSPCC; UK)

Website: http://www.nspcc.org.uk/preventing-abuse/child-abuse-and-neglect/female-genital-mutilation-fgm/)

FGM Helpline: 0800 028 3550 (if calling from the U.S., dial 011-44-800-028-3550)

E-mail: fgmhelp@nspcc.org.uk

The leading children's charity fighting to end child abuse in the UK and Channel Islands, NSPCC helps children who've been abused to rebuild their lives, protect those at risk, and find the best ways of preventing abuse from ever happening.

U.S. Department of State

(888) 407-4747

The U.S. Department of State's highest priority overseas is the protection and welfare of U.S. citizens. If you or someone you know is a U.S. citizen and could be or has been a victim of vacation cutting or forced marriage overseas, call the U.S. Embassy/Consulate nearest you.

U.S. Department of State's Office of Global Women's Issues:

http://www.state.gov/s/gwi/

The U.S. State Department's Office of Global Women's Issues, led by Ambassador-at-Large Catherine M. Russell, works to make certain that women's issues are totally integrated into the creation and carrying out of U.S. foreign policy. The Office of Global Women's Issues endeavors to advance the status of women and girls in U.S. foreign policy in order to improve health, nutrition, and gender equality. The office is also building on its efforts to compile and publish data to be used to help promote gender equality and improve the status of girls and women around the world. On February 6, 2015, Ambassador Russell spearheaded the State Department's first ever social media campaign on FGM/C using #TogetherForZero and #endFGM/C and calling for everyone around the world to stand up for zero tolerance of FGC every day. Ambassador Russell believes that tackling FGM/C is a top priority for her office. Ambassador Russell and the Office of Global Women's Issues' work can be followed on Twitter (twitter.com/AmbCathyRussell) and on the

Activist citizens such as these editors and designers at Rosen Publishing took to social media on Zero Tolerance Day to express their opposition to FGC, their commitment to seeing the practice eradicated, and their solidarity with survivors and at-risk girls and women.

State Department's blog (http://blogs.state.gov/stories/2015/02/05/international-day-zero-tolerance-female-genital-mutilation-cutting).

If You Have Had This Procedure

Many women who have been cut were emotionally traumatized by the ordeal, even if they do not remember the details. Women and girls who live in immigrant communities where cutting is traditional are surrounded by a larger community where the practice is unknown, may be particularly uneasy about discussing their condition. Gynecologic exams, being touched in the genital area, or even discussing "female problems" can trigger long-repressed fears and feelings. Questionnaires and interviews with women in the Birmingham project in England showed that those who had been cut were reluctant to seek the women's health information they needed.

It might help relieve fears of talking about personal health questions or problems to review medical information online before seeing a doctor. Many organizations support the elimination of female genital cutting and provide support to its victims. These same organizations can also provide important health and psychological counseling information and links to other resources. The resource you are reading includes a list of helpful organizations and websites.

Online sources might be able to help locate medical professionals in your area who have knowledge of or training related to female genital cutting. Look for a health professional who is familiar with the medical problems common among girls and women who have undergone the various types of genital cutting. If no one with this type of experience is available, you should ask your primary health care provider for a referral.

Reconstructive Surgery

Promising surgical procedures are giving hope to those who have already undergone female genital cutting. As reported in the U.N. publication *African Renewal Online* in 2013, more doctors than ever before are being trained in reconstruction techniques to help victims of infibulation and clitoridectomy.[1] Dr. Marci Bowers, a gynecologist who performs such surgeries, reports that the scarring and frequent infections that also result from cutting cause many women to live in constant pain. Dr. Bowers notes that by surgically reversing infibulation, women are able to pass urine and menstrual blood normally for the first time. The surgery is extremely effective in reducing pain. Reconstruction for patients who have undergone certain kinds of genital cutting is not new, but it is not available to millions of women who live in remote areas.[2]

French surgeon Dr. Pierre Foldès has developed a technique to reconstruct the clitoris. Although the visible part of a normal clitoris appears quite small, the organ is actually much larger below the surface. Surgery developed by Dr. Foldès involves removing scar tissue to expose the nerves hidden beneath it and then grafting on fresh tissue. In a 2012 article in the medical journal *The Lancet*, Dr. Foldès reported having operated on almost three thousand women between 1998 and 2009. His team followed up on patients one year after surgery, and most reported a lessening of pain and an increase in clitoral pleasure.[3]

Dr. Foldès has been training other surgeons in the use of his techniques. Among these is

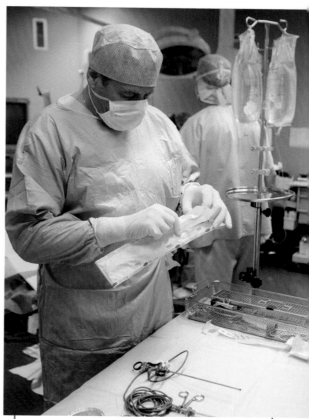

French urologist Pierre Foldès developed a technique to repair damage and restore sensation to women and girls who have undergone genital cutting. He continues to treat women in France successfully and has taught the procedure to doctors in other countries, including the United States.

WHAT ONE PERSON CAN DO

Houston attorney Donna Valverde learned about female genital cutting when she became close to the nurse who was caring for Valverde's ailing father. The nurse, Magdalene, a native of Sierra Leone, was cut at the age of fifteen. Magdalene suffered numerous physical problems and mental anguish from being cut. She fled her native country because she didn't want her daughters to suffer as she had.

Deeply affected by what Magdalene told her about female genital cutting, Donna Valverde set out to educate others about the practice and to help victims and those at risk. Valverde began researching female genital cutting and made several trips to Africa to learn from circumcisers, victims, and those fighting the practice. From this research, she created a feature-length documentary, *Healing Magdalene*, to educate others about female genital cutting and efforts to end the practice. The film was completed in 2012 and has been shown in numerous film festivals and selected cities.

The Valvisions Foundation was created in 2007 with the initial focus on aiding victims of female genital cutting and providing education about the practice. The foundation has an office in Kampala, which oversees programs in Kenya and Uganda. These programs include scholarships to cover housing and education for girls (some of whom become outcasts after resisting being cut or arranged child marriages). Girl's Choice Clubs in local high schools help participants learn about becoming confident young women and making choices about their bodies. Students participate in coming-of-age ceremonies that include candle lighting and spoken words, rather than cutting. Plans are being made to make these clubs coeducational in the future.

Ms. Valverde learned that many African girls must discontinue their education when menstruation begins because they are unable to pay for sanitary products. To help, Valvisions Foundation began the MC Project to provide long-lasting, reusable menstrual cups to young women. Later, the foundation began working with a hospital in Africa to supply menstrual cups for use by incontinent victims of certain fistulas.

Dr. Bowers, who works in California and volunteers in Africa. The procedure is also available in New York State, where it is sponsored by the organization Clitoraid. Clitoraid is also active in Africa and working to open a hospital in Burkina Faso dedicated to restorative surgery. Another organization, the Campaign Against Female Genital Mutilation (CAGeM), was organized in 1998 by a group of women doctors in Africa. CAGeM is building a "Restoration Hospital" in southern Nigeria to provide free reconstruction services to victims of genital cutting. The efforts of such organizations are extremely important, as few African women can afford to travel and pay for surgery abroad.

Physical restoration alone cannot heal the pain and damage of genital cutting. Many cut women suffer from a sense of shame. They cannot forget the terrifying experience of being held down and cut. The post-traumatic stress of their experience, plus the constant pain, mean that many women fear being touched "down there" by anyone, even a husband or doctor. Following reconstructive surgery, the patient may be pain free and able to experience sexual pleasure but mentally unprepared for new physical sensations. Doctors who perform clitoral reconstruction are aware of the need for counseling and possible sexual therapy. New sensations may be reminders of past pain. A lifelong fear of being touched cannot be eliminated through surgery. Although restorative surgery is not always successful, it offers hope to those who have been cut.

In the Chicago area, the organization Forma offers individual and group counseling tailored to women affected by female genital cutting. The African Women's Health Center associated with Brigham and Women's Hospital in Boston conducts workshops to help those suffering from FGC and educate health care providers in treating them. However, one does not have to find an expert trained in the effects of genital cutting to get help. Depression, sexual problems, anger, and a sense of shame and self-loathing are problems that arise from many situations. Ask your school counselor or primary health professional for a referral to someone who can provide help in dealing with such emotions. A therapist trained in family violence or child abuse, for example, might be able to provide helpful counseling.

What You Can Do

Crusaders such as Efua Dorkenoo and activists like Molly Melching and Donna Valverde have done much to further the cause of eliminating the practice of female genital cutting. An Internet search shows that many organizations around the world are focused on this issue. But millions of people who live outside of the countries where female genital cutting is prevalent remain unaware of the practice. Raising awareness is important because changes in laws

A group of Ethiopian girls celebrate being the first generation in their village not to undergo genital cutting. The girls' mothers are not willing to have their daughters cut, having realized the mental and physical risks of the practice through their own experiences.

and customs have accelerated in recent decades because of public awareness and public pressure.

The elimination of the practice of female genital cutting around the world is an important cause that merits public attention. Whether you are interested in furthering this cause as a woman, as an activist, or because of personal experience, your help is needed. Many organizations offer educational materials suitable for young people. Although the subject is extremely sensitive, it could be included as part of a broader community awareness program on human rights or child protection.

Organizations working to end the practice of female genital cutting need money to further educational efforts, and help those trying to escape being cut or those who are already affected. For many organizations, female genital cutting is only one issue among several that they are working on. Ending female genital cutting is an important way to empower women and girls and ensure their basic human rights. The same women and girls who are subjected to female genital cutting are often victimized in other ways as well. They may be forced into child marriages or denied an education. Poverty may make it impossible for them to get the physical and mental health services they need. They are often denied the freedom to make the most basic decisions about their lives. If you, your school, or your organization is looking for a way to make a difference in the world, consider raising money to help organizations to empower these women and girls. Is it possible to end the practice of female genital cutting in your lifetime? Dedicated, persistent individuals have accelerated the movement to change customs and lives, yet there is still much to be done.

CHASTE Describing someone who abstains from sexual intercourse, particularly outside of marriage.

CLITORIS A small, sensitive part of the female genitals, found at the upper portion of the vulva.

DISSEMINATE To spread something, such as an idea or practice, over a wide area.

ENDOMETRIOSIS A disease that occurs when tissue like that of the lining of the uterus grows in other parts of the body. The immune system does not act correctly in response to this disease.

ETHNIC GROUP A group that shares a common national or cultural tradition.

EXCISION The surgical cutting or removal of a part of the body.

FISTULA An abnormal passage or hole between the vaginal wall and the bladder or between the vagina and the rectum.

GENITALIA Human or animal organs of sexual reproduction. Also called genitals.

GYNECOLOGIC Relating to the medical specialty that deals with conditions found only in women and girls, particularly relating to reproductive organs.

HEMORRHAGE An escape of blood from a ruptured blood vessel.

INCONTINENCE Inability to control one's urination or defecation.

INFIBULATION The narrowing of the vagina's opening by cutting and bringing together the labia minora and/or the labia majora to make a kind of seal, with or without excision of the clitoris. In most cases, the cut edges of the labia are stitched together.

INTACT Complete; not damaged in any way, by cutting, for example.

OPPRESSION Prolonged cruel or unjust treatment or control of someone or something.

POULTICE A soft mass of material (typically plant material) applied to the body to relieve soreness and inflammation.

PREVALENT Widespread in a particular area or at a particular time.

PUBERTY Period during which adolescent bodies mature sexually and become capable of reproduction.

REPRESS To inhibit the natural development of something or self-expression of someone; not to acknowledge thoughts, feelings, or desires.

RESTORATIVE SURGERY Treatment or medical procedures designed to restore a damaged part of the body to its original form and/or function.

SEPSIS Harmful bacteria or toxins in tissue, typically through infection of a wound.

SEXUAL INTERCOURSE Sexual contact involving insertion of a man's erect penis into a woman's vagina.

TRAUMA A deeply disturbing experience and the emotional shock that may result from it; the medical term for a physical injury.

VULVA The external female reproductive organs.

The AHA Foundation
130 7th Avenue, Suite 236
New York, NY 10011
Website: http://theahafoundation.org
FGC: http://www.theahafoundation.org/female-genital-mutilation
The AHA Foundation is the leading organization working to end
honor violence that shames, hurts, or kills thousands of women
and girls in the United States each year and puts millions more
at risk. It ensures that women and girls of all races, cultures,
religions, and beliefs who are facing honor violence have a way
out and that survivors get the help they need to thrive. The
AHA Foundation has consistently advocated for the expansion
of FGC legislation to include procedures performed abroad.
The AHA Foundation has undertaken a campaign to encour-
age state legislators in the twenty-nine states without law
against it to pass criminal prohibitions against FGC. Ongoing
initiatives include educating service providers on the risks of
FGC and the reality of vacation cutting.

Amnesty International Canada
1992 Yonge Street
Toronto, ON MSS1Z7
Canada
(416) 363-9933
Website: http://www.anmesty.ca
Amnesty International is a worldwide organization dedicated to
protecting and promoting human rights. The organization
works to help individuals whose human rights have been
violated, to raise public awareness about human rights
violations, and to bring about changes in laws.

Amnesty International USA Headquarters
5 Penn Plaza, Sixteenth Floor
New York, NY 10001
(212) 807-8400
Website: http://www.amnestyusa.org
Amnesty International USA has numerous articles listed on one
    of its website's pages (http://www.amnestyusa.org/search/
    node/female%20genital%20cutting) involving the
    organization's work to help end the practice of FGC. It also
    describes actions that people can take to in end violence
    against women (http://www.amnestyusa.org/our-work/
    issues/women-s-rightsviolence-against-women
    ?utm_source=feature&utm_medium=homepage&utm
    _campaign=IVAWA).

Canadian Women's Foundation
133 Richmond Street West, Suite 504
Toronto, ON MSH 2L3
Canada
(866) 293-4483
Website: http://www.canadianwomen.org
The Canadian Women's Foundation is working to stop violence
    against women, to improve their economic situations, and to
    empower girls. The organization sponsors education and
    mentoring programs to aid girls and women at risk. The
    organization also provides support to victims of violence
    and human trafficking.

Center for Reproductive Rights
120 Wall Street

New York, NY 10005

(917) 637-3600

Website: http://www.reproductiverights.org

Articles on FGC: http://www.reproductiverights.org/search/
google/female%20genital%20cutting?query=female%20
genital%20cutting&cx=013411022521635236165%3Aqn
myx__l41c&cof=FORID%3A11&sitesearch=

The Center for Reproductive Rights is a global legal advocacy
organization dedicated to reproductive rights. The organization works by bringing legal action, documenting abuses,
and shaping government policy around the world.

Change.org

Website: https://www.change.org

Change.org is a petition platform for people who want to begin
campaigns to help transform communities around the world.
See https://www.change.org/search?utf8=%E2%9C%93&q
=female+genital+mutilation for a list of various petitions to
end FGM/C.

Equality Now

PO Box 20646, Columbus Circle Station

New York, NY 10023

(212) 586-0906

Website: http://www.equalitynow.org

FGC: http://www.equalitynow.org/fgm

Equality Now advocates for the human rights of women and
girls by increasing public awareness. The organization works
around the world to ensure that governments enact and
enforce laws to uphold the rights of women and girls.

Female genital cutting is one area of focus for the organization.

Forma
4753 North Broadway, Suite 509
Chicago, IL 60640
(877) 603-3833
Website: http://formafgc.org
Forma offers culturally sensitive clinical services to women and
families who are affected by female genital cutting in the
Chicago region. It provides information and education around
the physical and psychological effects for women who have
been cut, and it serves as a link between women and
professionals who provide services around the United States.
The website offers personal stories and serves as a place to
share experiences, information, and encouragement.

FORWARD (Foundation for Women's Health, Research and
Development) International
Suite 2.1 Chandelier Building, 8 Scrubs Lane
London NW10 6RB
United Kingdom
44 (0) 20 8960 4000
Website: http:// www.forwarduk.org.uk
Articles on FGC: http://www.forwarduk.org.uk/?s=female+genit
al+mutilation&submit=Go
FORWARD, founded by African women in the United Kingdom,
is dedicated to advancing and safeguarding the sexual and
reproductive health and rights of African girls and women.
FORWARD works with individuals, communities, and

organizations in an effort to eliminate female genital cutting, child marriage, and fistulas.

Office of Global Women's Issues
U.S. Department of State
2201 C Street NW
Washington, DC 20520
(202) 647-4000
Website: www.state.gov/s/gwi/
Articles on FGC: http://search.state.gov/search?q=female+geni
tal+cutting&site=state_en_stategov&client=state_en_
stategov&output=xml_no_dtd&proxystylesheet=state_en_
stategov&filter=0&entqr=3&lr=lang_en&oe=utf8&ie=utf8&get
fields=*&search-button=Search
The Office of Global Women's Issues, under Ambassador-at-Large for Global Women's Issues Catherine M. Russell, has spoken out against female genital mutilation and cutting. Russell launched the first ever social media campaign on FGM/C using #TogetherForZero and #endFGMC on February 6, 2015. The Office for Global Women's Issues has made zero tolerance of FGM/C one of its primary missions globally.

Safe Hands for Girls
Atlanta, Georgia
(678) 306-6717
Website: http://safehandsforgirls.org
This nonprofit organization, founded by Jaha Dukureh, works to protect girls and women from FGM/C and provides support services for women who have had FGC. It also is committed to ending all violence against women, specifically FGM/C.

The survivor-led organization can also be followed on Twitter at https://twitter.com/safehands4girls along with its founder at https://twitter.com/JahaENDFGM.

Sanctuary for Families
Immigration Intervention Project (IIP)
Department of Political Science
Rutgers, the State University of New Jersey
89 George Street
New Brunswick, NJ 08901-1411
(212) 349-6009, ext. 288
Website: http://www.sanctuaryforfamilies.org
The Immigration Intervention Project (IIP) provides immigrant victims of domestic and gender-based violence (including female genital cutting) with legal services that allow them to formalize their immigration status in the United States. Sanctuary staff and pro bono attorneys assist clients with immigration relief by filing Violence Against Women Act (VAWA) self-petitions and battered spouse waivers, as well as applications for asylum, special immigrant juvenile status (for abused immigrant youth in the foster care system), U nonimmigrant status (for immigrant crime victims who cooperate in the prosecution of certain gender-motivated crimes), and T nonimmigrant status (for trafficking victims). The IIP also provides legal representation to victims threatened with deportation. New initiatives include the legal representation of victims of sex trafficking, as well as detained victims of domestic and gender-based violence.

Tostan
2121 Decatur Place NW
Washington, DC 20008
(202) 299-1156
Website: http://www.tostan.org
FGC: http://www.tostan.org/female-genital-cutting
Founded by Molly Melching, Tostan works to provide dignity
  to the lives of all people. It particularly focuses its efforts
  on empowering African communities and on partnering
  with them to ensure healthy and hygienic practices. It
  also reaches out to educate communities about the
  health risks of harmful practices such as FGC.

United Nations Children's Fund (UNICEF)
UNICEF House
3 United Nations Plaza
New York, NY 10017
(212) 326-7000
Website: http://www.unicef.org
Articles on FGC: http://www.unicefusa.org/search/
  node?search=female%20genital%20cutting#gsc.
  tab=0&gsc.q=female%20genital%20cutting&gsc.page=1
UNICEF is the world's leading advocate for children. The
  organization works with 190 countries to promote the
  protection, education, and social inclusion of children.
  UNICEF agencies conduct research and help develop
  programs that support the welfare of women and
  children.

United States Department of Women's Services, Office of
    Women's Health
200 Independence Avenue SW
Washington, DC 20201
(800) 994-9662
Website: http://www.womenshealth.gov
This federal government office provides leadership and
    coordination to improve the health of women and girls
    through policy, education, and model programs. The
    website provides information and e-publications on FGC
    as well as many other topics relating to female health.

Valvisions Foundation
2700 Post Oak Boulevard, Suite 1400
Houston, TX 77056
(281) 657-3315
Website: http://www.valvisions.org
Valvisions Foundation is dedicated to fighting social ills. The
    foundation has funded programs to raise public awareness
    about female genital cutting. It also sponsors scholarships
    and educational and health outreach programs for girls in
    Kenya and Uganda.

World Health Organization (WHO)
Avenue Appia 20
1211 Geneva 27
Switzerland
41 22 791 21 11
Website: http://www.who.int

Articles on FGC: http://search.who.int/search?q=female+gen
    ital+cutting&ie=utf8&site=who&client=_en_r&proxystyle
    sheet=_en_r&output=xml_no_dtd&oe=utf8&getfields=
    doctype
The WHO is the authority that directs and coordinates health
    matters within the United Nations organization. The WHO
    provides leadership on global health issues. It also moni-
    tors health trends and provides technical support to
    countries.

Websites
Because of the changing nature of Internet links, Rosen
Publishing has developed an online list of websites related to
the subject of this book. This site is updated regularly. Please
use this link to access the list:

http://www.rosenlinks.com/CVAW/Cut

FOR FURTHER READING

Abdi, Hawa. *Keeping Hope Alive.* New York, NY: Grand Central Publishing, 2013.

Alexander, Linda Lewis, Judith H. LaRosa, Helaine Bader, Susan Garfield, and William James Alexander. *New Dimensions in Women's Health*. 6th ed. Burlington, MA: Jones & Bartlett Learning, 2014.

Ali, Nujood, and Delphine Minoui. *I Am Nujood, Age 10 and Divorced.* New York, NY: Three Rivers Press, 2010.

Blumen, Lorna, Natalie Evans, and Anne Rucchetto. *Girls' Respect Groups: An Innovative Program to Empower Young Women and Build Self-Esteem.* Toronto, ON: Camberley Press, 2009.

Boyle, Elizabeth Heger. *Female Genital Cutting: Cultural Conflict in the Global Community.* Baltimore, MD: Johns Hopkins University Press, 2005.

Comfort, Momoh, ed. *Female Genital Mutilation*. Oxford, UK: Radcliffe Publishing, 2006.

Dirie, Waris. *Desert Children.* London, UK: Virago, 2008.

Dirie, Waris. *Desert Dawn.* London, UK: Virago, 2004.

Dirie, Waris, and Cathleen Miller. *Desert Flower: The Extraordinary Journey of a Desert Nomad.* Orlando, FL: William Morrow Paperbacks, 2011.

Dorkenoo, Efua. *Cutting the Rose: Female Genital Mutilation: The Practice & Its Prevention*. Austin, TX: Harry Ransom Humanities Research Center, 1996.

Foundation for Women's Health, Research and Development. "Female Genital Mutilation: Frequently Asked Questions: A Campaigner's Guide for Young People." 2012. Retrieved December 4, 2014 (http://www.forwarduk.org.uk/fgm -frequently-asked-questions).

Hernlund, Ylva, and Bettina Shell-Duncan, ed. *Transcultural Bodies: Female Genital Cutting in Global Context.* Piscataway, NJ: Rutgers University Press, 2007.

Hirsi Ali, Ayaan. *The Caged Virgin: An Emancipation Proclamation for Women and Islam.* New York, NY: Free Press, 2006.

Hirsi Ali, Ayaan. *Infidel.* New York, NY: Atria, 2008.

Hirsi Ali, Ayaan. *Nomad: From Islam to America: A Personal Journey Through the Clash of Civilizations.* New York, NY: Free Press, 2010.

Hirsi Ali, Ayaan, and Theo van Gogh. *Submission: Part I.* Film short. 2004.

Klugman, Jeni, Lucia Hanmer, and Sarah Twigg. *Voice and Agency: Empowering Women and Girls for Shared Prosperity.* Washington, DC: World Bank Publications, 2014.

Lucy, Janet. *Moon Mother, Moon Daughter.* Santa Barbara, CA: Publishing by the Seas, 2012.

Mire, Soraya. *The Girl with Three Legs: A Memoir.* Chicago, IL: Lawrence Hill Books, 2011.

Molloy, Aimee. *Molly Melching's Journey to Help Millions of African Women and Girls Triumph.* New York, NY: HarperOne, 2014.

Nyangweso-Wangila, Mary. *Female Genital Cutting in Industrialized Countries: Mutilation or Cultural Tradition?* Santa Barbara, CA: Praeger, 2014.

Rodger, Ellen. *Human Rights Activist.* New York, NY: Crabtree Publishing, 2010.

Rogo, Khama, Tshiya Subayi, and Nahid Toubia. *Female Genital Cutting, Women's Health, and Development* (World Bank Working Papers). Washington, DC: World Bank Publications, 2007.

Ruglass, Lesia, and Kathleen Kendall-Tackett. *Psychology of Trauma 101.* New York, NY: Springer Publishing, 2014.

Skaine, Rosemarie. *Female Genital Mutilation: Legal, Cultural, and Medical Issues.* Jefferson, NC: McFarland, 2005.

Steffen, Charles G. *Mutilating Khalid: The Symbolic Politics of Female Genital Cutting.* Trenton, NJ: Red Sea Press, 2011.

Thurow, Roger. *The Last Hungry Season: A Year in an African Farm Community on the Brink of Change.* New York, NY: Public Affairs, 2013.

Todres, Nadia. *Rising Up: Empowering Adolescent Girls Through the Arts in Haiti.* Piéton-Ville, Haiti: Nota Bene Editions, 2014.

Valverde, Donna. *Healing Magdalene* Film. Houston, TX: Valvisions Foundation, 2013.

van de Kolk, Bessel. *The Body Keeps the Score: Brain, Mind, and Body in the Healing of Trauma.* New York, NY: Viking, 2014.

Walker, Alice. *Possessing the Secret of Joy.* New York, NY: Harcourt Brace & Company, 1992.

Walker, Alice, and Pratibha Parmar. *Warrior Marks: Female Genital Mutilation and the Sexual Blinding of Women.* New York, NY: Harcourt Brace & Company, 1993.

Althaus, Frances A. "Female Circumcision: Rite of Passage Or Violation of Rights?" Special Report. Guttmacher Institute. International Family Planning Perspectives. Volume 23, No. 3, September 1997. Retrieved March 31, 2015 (http://www .guttmacher.org/pubs/journals/2313097.html), pp. 130–133.

Blackledge, Catherine. *The Story of V: A Natural History of Female Sexuality.* New Brunswick, NJ: Rutgers University Press, 2004.

Boston Women's Health Book Collective. *Our Bodies, Ourselves.* 40th anniversary ed. New York, NY: Touchstone, 2011.

Crompton, Paul. "Female Genital Mutilation in U.S. Sparks Warnings." *Al Arabiya News.* Retrieved October 15, 2014 (http://english.alarabiya.net/en/perspective/features/2014 /06/28/).

Eltahawy, Mona. "Fighting Female Genital Mutilation," *New York Times*, November 16, 2014. Retrieved March 24, 2015 (http://www.nytimes.com/2014/11/17/opinion/fighting -female-genital-mutilation.html).

Equality Now. "Female Genital Mutilation in the U.S. Fact Sheet." Updated February 2015. Retrieved May 12, 2014 (http://www.equalitynow.org/sites/default/files/EN_FAQ _FGM_in_US.pdf).

Foldès, Pierre, B. Cuzin, and A. Andro. "Reconstructive Surgery After Female Genital Mutilation: A Prospective Cohort Study." *The Lancet.* Retrieved October 29, 2014 (http:// www.thelancet.com/journals/lancet/article/PIIS0140 -6736(12)60400-0/abstract).

Foundation for Women's Health, Research and Development. "New Estimates on FGM in England and Wales by Equality

Now and City University London." Retrieved August 28,
2014 (http://www.equalitynow.org/print/2267).

Foundation for Women's Health, Research and Development.
"Voices of Child Brides and Child Mothers in Tanzania: A
PEER Report on Child Marriage." Retrieved November 4,
2014 (http://www.forwarduk.org.uk/resources/publications).

Foundation for Women's Health, Research and Development.
"Women's Experiences, Perceptions and Attitudes of
Female Genital Mutilation: The Bristol PEER Study." 2010.
Retrieved September 25, 2014.

Ismail, Edna Adan. "Female Genital Mutilation Survey in
Somaliland at the Edna Adan Maternity and Teaching
Hospital, Hargeisa, Somaliland 2002 to 2009." Edna Adan
University Hospital.org. Retrieved January 2, 2015 (http://
www.ednahospital.org/female-genital-mutilation.pdf).

Khan, Saira. "Trying to Rebuild Women's Bodies After
'Female Circumcision.'" The Atlantic, May 2014.
Retrieved October 17, 2014 (http://www.theatlantic.com/
health/archive/2014/05/reversing-female-genital
-mutilation/361540).

Kristof, Nicholas D., and Sheryl WuDunn. Half the Sky: Turning
Oppression into Opportunity for Women Worldwide. New
York, NY: Knopf, 2009.

Lorenzi, Rossella. "How Did Female Genital Mutilation Begin?"
Discovery News, December 10, 2012. Retrieved December
31, 2014 (http://news.discovery.com/human/female-genital
-mutilation-begin-121210.htm).

Mather, Mark, and Charlotte Feldman-Jacobs. "Women and
Girls at Risk of Female Genital Mutilation/Cutting in the
United States." Population Reference Bureau, February

2015. Retrieved February 6, 2015 (http://www.prb.org/
Publications/Articles/2015/us-fgmc.aspx).

Meade, Teresa A., and Merry E. Wiesner-Hanks. *A Companion to Gender History*. Malden, MA: Blackwell Publishing, 2004.

Monger, George P. *Marriage Customs of the World: An Encyclopedia of Dating Customs and Wedding Traditions*. Expanded 2nd ed. Santa Barbara, CA: ABC-CLIO, 2013.

Pearson, Catherine. "Female Hysteria: 7 Crazy Things People Used to Believe About the Ladies' Disease." Huffington Post, November 21, 2013. Retrieved January 2015 (http://www.huffingtonpost.com/2013/11/21/female-hysteria_n_4298060.html).

Sambira, Jocelyne. "Reconstructive Surgery Brings Hope to Survivors of Genital Cutting." Africa Renewal Online. Retrieved October 29, 2014 (http://www.un.org/africarenewal/magazine/january-2013/reconstructive-surgery-brings-hope-survivors-genital-cutting).

Sanctuary for Families. "Female Genital Mutilation in the United States: Protecting Girls and Women in the U.S. from FGM and Vacation Cutting." New York, NY: Sanctuary for Families, 2013. Retrieved January 2, 2015 (http://www.sanctuaryforfamilies.org/storage/sanctuary/documents/report_onfgm_w_cover.pdf).

Smith, Bonnie G. *Women's History in Global Perspective*. Urbana, IL: University of Illinois Press, 2005.

Spirited Pictures. "Female Genital Mutilation: A Change Has Begun." Retrieved October 22, 2014 (http://www.forwarduk.org.uk).

Summers, Leigh. *Bound to Please: A History of the Victorian Corset*. Oxford, UK: Berg, 2001.

Topping, Alexandra. "FGM: First Suspects to be Charged Appear in Court." *Guardian*, April 15, 2014. Retrieved September 18, 2014 (http://www.theguardian.com/society/2014/apr/15/fgm-first-suspects-charged-court).

Turkewitz, Julie. "A Fight as U.S. Girls Face Genital Cutting Abroad." *New York Times*, June 10, 2014. Retrieved March 30, 2015 (http://www.nytimes.com/2014/06/11/us/a-fight-as-us-girls-face-genital-cutting-abroad.html?_r=0).

United Nations Children's Fund. "Female Genital Mutilation/Cutting." Child Protection from Violence, Exploitation and Abuse, October 31, 2014. Retrieved March 31, 2015 (http://www.unicef.org/protection/57929_58002.html).

United Nations Children's Fund. "Female Genital Mutilation/Cutting: A Statistical Overview and Exploration of the Dynamics of Change." Retrieved September 10, 2014 (http://www.unicef.org/media/files/FGCM_Lo_res.pdf).

United Nations News Centre. "UN Committee Approves First-ever Text Calling for End to Female Genital Mutilation." November 28, 2012. Retrieved May 11, 2015 (http://www.un.org/apps/news/story.asp?NewsID=43625#.VKb4yFqRYyE).

United Nations Population Fund. "Driving Forces in Outlawing the Practice of Female Genital Mutilation/Cutting in Kenya, Uganda and Guinea-Bissau." October 2013. Retrieved October 14, 2014 (http://www.unfpa.org/female-genital-mutilation).

Valverde, Donna. *Healing Magdalene* Film. Houston, TX: Valvisions Foundation, 2013.

Valverde, Donna. Interview with the author, October 2014.

World Health Organization. "Eliminating Female Genital
    Mutilation: An Interagency Statement: OHCHR, UNAIDS,
    UNDP, UNECA, UNESCO, UNFPA, UNHCR, UNIFEM,
    WHO." 2008. Retrieved September 22, 2014 (http://www
    .unfpa.org/sites/default/files/pub-pdf/eliminating_fgm.pdf).
World Health Organization. "Female Genital Mutilation Fact
    Sheet." Retrieved October 20, 2014 (http://www.who.int/
    mediacentre/factsheets/fs241/en).
World Health Organization. "Global Strategy to Stop Health
    Care Providers from Performing Female Genital Mutilation."
    Retrieved September 15, 2014 (http://whglibdoc.who.int).

SOURCE NOTES

Introduction

1. Spirited Pictures, "Female Genital Mutilation: A Change Has Begun," https://vimeo.com/spiritedpictures.
2. World Health Organization (WHO), "Female Genital Mutilation Fact Sheet," http://www.who.int/mediacentre/factsheets/fs241/en.
3. Mark Mather and Charlotte Feldman-Jacobs, "Women and Girls at Risk of Female Genital Mutilation/Cutting in the United States," Population Reference Bureau, February 2015.
4. United Nations Children's Fund (UNICEF), "Female Genital Mutilation/Cutting: A Statistical Overview and Exploration of the Dynamics of Change," (hereafter, UNICEF 2013), http://www.unicef.org/malaysia/FGCM_Lo_res.pdf, p. 114.
5. Sanctuary for Families, Female Genital Mutilation in the United States: Protecting Girls and Women in the U.S. from FGM and Vacation Cutting," http://www.sanctuaryforfamilies.org/storage/sanctuary/documents/report_onfgm_w_cover.pdf, p. ii.

Chapter 1

1. Equality Now, "Female Genital Mutilation in the U.S. Fact Sheet," http://www.equalitynow.org/sites/default/files/EN_FAQ_FGM_in_US.pdf, p. 1.
2. UNICEF 2013, p. 7.
3. Rossella Lorenzi, "How Did Female Genital Mutilation Begin?" http://news.discovery.com/human/female-genital-mutilation-begin-121210.htm.

4. Mona Eltahawy, "Fighting Female Genital Mutilation," *New York Times*, November 16, 2014, http://www.nytimes.com/2014/11/17/opinion/fighting-female-genital-mutilation.html.

5. WHO, FGM Fact Sheet.

6. George P. Monger, *Marriage Customs of the World: An Encyclopedia of Dating Customs and Wedding Traditions* (Santa Barbara, CA: ABC-CLIO, 2013), p. 142.

7. Catherine Pearson, "Female Hysteria: 7 Crazy Things People Used to Believe About the Ladies' Disease," Huffington Post, November 21, 2013, http://www.huffingtonpost.com/2013/11/21/female-hysteria_n_4298060.html.

8. WHO, FGM Fact Sheet.

9. UNICEF 2013, p. 23.

10. Sanctuary for Families, "Female Genital Mutilation in the United States: Protecting Girls and Women in the U.S. from FGM and Vacation Cutting," p. 7.

Chapter 2

1. WHO, FGM Fact Sheet.

2. Ibid.

3. Edna Adan Ismail, "Female Genital Mutilation Survey in Somaliland at the Edna Adan Maternity and Teaching Hospital, Hargeisa, Somaliland 2002 to 2009." Edna Adan University Hospital.org, http://www.ednahospital.org/female-genital-mutilation.pdf, p. 12.

4. WHO, "Global Strategy to Stop Health Care Providers from Performing Female Genital Mutilation," http://whglibdoc.who.int, p. 9.

5. WHO, FGM Fact Sheet.
6. Foundation for Women's Health, Research and Development (FORWARD), "Women's Experience, Perceptions and Attitudes of Female Genital Mutilation: The Bristol PEER Study," 2010, http://www.forwarduk.org.uk/wp-content/uploads/2014/12/Womens-Experiences-Perceptions-and-Attitudes-of-Female-Genital-Mutilation-The-Bristol-PEER-Study.pdf, p. 18.

Chapter 3

1. Foundation for Women's Health, Research and Development (FORWARD), "Women's Experiences, Perceptions and Attitudes of Female Genital Mutilation: The Bristol PEER Study," http://www.forwarduk.org.uk/wp-content/uploads/2014/12/Womens-Experiences-Perceptions-and-Attitudes-of-Female-Genital-Mutilation-The-Bristol-PEER-Study.pdf, pp.14–19.
2. World Health Organization, "Eliminating Female Genital Mutilation: An Interagency Statement: OHCHR, UNAIDS, UNDP, UNECA, UNESCO, UNFPA, UNHCR, UNIFEM, WHO," p. 6.
3. Foundation for Women's Health, Research and Development (FORWARD), "Women's Experiences, Perceptions and Attitudes of Female Genital Mutilation: The Bristol PEER Study," http://www.forwarduk.org.uk/wp-content/uploads/2014/12/Womens-Experiences-Perceptions-and-Attitudes-of-Female-Genital-Mutilation-The-Bristol-PEER-Study.pdf, p. 18.

4. United Nations Population Fund, "Driving forces in Outlawing the Practice of Female Genital Mutilation/ Cutting in Kenya, Uganda and Guinea-Bissau," October 2013, http://www.unfpa.org/female-genital -mutilation), p. 18.

5. Julie Turkewitz, "A Fight as U.S. Girls Face Genital Cutting Abroad," *New York Times*, June 10, 2014, http://www .nytimes.com/2014/06/11/us/a-fight-as-us-girls-face -genital-cutting-abroad.html?_r=0.

6. Ibid.

Chapter 4

1. UNICEF 2013, p. 10.

2. Frances A. Althaus, "Female Circumcision: Rite of Passage Or Violation of Rights?" Special Report, Guttmacher Institute, International Family Planning Perspectives, Volume 23, No. 3, September 1997, http://www.guttmacher.org/ pubs/journals/2313097.html, p. 132.

3. Ibid., p. 10.

4. Ibid.

5. Ibid., p. 11.

6. Ibid., p. 12.

7. United Nations News Centre, "UN Committee Approves First-ever Text Calling for End to Female Genital Mutilation," November 28, 2012, http://www.un.org/apps/news/story .asp?NewsID=43625#.VKb4yFqRYyE.

8. United Nations Populations Fund, National Legislation, http:// www.unfpa.org/topics/genderissues/fgm.

9. Alexandra Topping, "FGM: First Suspects to be Charged Appear in Court," *Guardian*, April 15, 2014, http://www .theguardian.com/society/2014/apr/15/fgm-first-suspects -charged-court.
10. Tostan, http://www.tostan.org.
11. UNICEF 2013, p. 89.
12. Ibid., p. 114.
13. United Nations Children's Fund, "Female Genital Mutilation/ Cutting," Child Protection from Violence, Exploitation and Abuse, October 31, 2014, http://www.unicef.org/protection /57929_58002.html.

Chapter 5

1. Jocelyne Sambira, "Reconstructive Surgery Brings Hope to Survivors of Genital Cutting," *African Renewal Online*, January 2013 http://www.un.org/africarenewal/magazine/january -2013/reconstructive-surgery-brings-hope-survivors -genital-cutting.
2. Ibid.
3. Pierre Foldès, B. Cuzin, and A. Andro, "Reconstructive Surgery After Female Genital Mutilation: A Prospective Cohort Study," *The Lancet*, July 14, 2012, http://www .thelancet.com/journals/lancet/article/PIIS0140-6736 (12)60400-0/abstract.

A

Africa, 10, 11, 15, 19, 21, 31, 45, 51, 53, 59, 72–73
African Renewal Online, 70
African Women's Health Center, 74
AHA Foundation, 66–67
American Psychiatric Association, 18

B

Benin, 56
Bowers, Marci, 70–71, 73
Burkina Faso, 45, 73

C

Campaign Against Female Genital Mutilation (CAGeM), 66, 73
Central African Republic, 44, 56,
chastity belts, 18
childbirth, 24, 28, 29, 30, 32, 36, 38
circumcisers, 25, 29, 37, 40, 49, 72
Clitoraid, 73
clitoridectomy, 18, 25, 70
clitoris, 17, 18, 24, 25, 34–35, 71
Cutting the Rose, 51

D

Diagnostic and Statistical Manual of Mental Disorders, 19
Djibouti, 44
Dorkenoo, Efua, 51, 74
Dukureh, Jaha, 25, 63–64

E

Egypt, 15, 41, 44
Equality Now, 20, 48, 50, 60, 67
excision, 25

F

Foundation for Women's Health, Research and Development (FORWARD), 10, 33, 36, 38, 51, 60
"female circumcision," 12, 14
female genital cutting (FGC)
    complications of, 8, 29, 30–31, 33, 42
    cultural tradition of, 31, 34–41, 43, 49, 55, 56, 58, 59, 61, 67
    health consequences of, 10, 11, 14, 24, 28, 31, 34, 53, 59, 70, 76
    laws against, 10, 11, 37, 42–48, 49, 59, 61–62, 75
    myths and facts about, 21
    organizations working to combat it, 10, 13, 20, 33, 34, 39, 43, 47, 50, 53, 60, 62–69, 73–76
    raising awareness about, 10, 51, 53, 65, 74–76
    role of religion in, 21, 41–42, 67
    statistics/data on, 10, 11, 15, 31, 56, 59–60, 63, 68
    in the United States, 10, 11, 20, 31, 37, 47, 48
Female Genital Mutilation: A Change Has Begun, 8
fistulas, 29, 30, 31, 59, 73
flesh-eating disease, 28, 30
Foldès, Pierre, 71
foot-binding, 17–18

G

Gambia, 25, 41, 53, 56, 63
Ghana, 41, 51
Guinea, 44
Guinea-Bissau, 39

H

Half the Sky, 52
Hawaa, 44
Healing Magdalene, 38, 72
health care professionals, 14, 31, 57, 61–62, 70, 74
hepatitis, 28, 30
HIV, 14, 30
human rights, 22, 46, 47, 48, 51–53, 55, 66, 67, 76
hymen, 24, 25
hysteria, 18

I

incontinence, 31
infections, 28, 29, 30–31, 33, 57, 70
infibulation, 17, 25, 28, 29, 36, 44, 70–71
Inter-African Committee on Tribal Practices Affecting the Health of Women and Children, 14
intercourse, 17, 18, 23, 24, 28, 30, 31, 33, 34–35, 36, 57
International Day of Zero Tolerance for Female Genital Mutilation, 47
Iraq, 56

K

Kenya, 44, 45, 47, 56, 72
Ki-moon, Ban, 65

L

labia majora, 24, 25
labia minora, 24, 25
Liberia, 56

M

Maendeleo Ya Wanawake Organization, 47
male circumcision, 12–14
MC Project, 73
Melching, Molly, 51, 52–53, 74
Middle East, 10, 11, 15, 19
Mohamed, Fahma, 64–65

N

National Society for the Prevention of Cruelty to Children (NSPCC), 67–68
New York Times, 15, 37, 41, 51
Nigeria, 56, 73

P

perineum, 24
Population Reference Bureau, 10
post-traumatic stress disorder (PTSD), 31, 32
pregnancy, 23, 36

R

reconstructive surgery, 70–71, 73–74
reinfibulation, 32
rites of passage, 37, 38–39, 42, 47

S

Safe Hands for Girls, 63
Sanctuary for Families, 66
Senegal, 41, 45, 47, 52
Sierra Leone, 72
Sinim Mira Nassique, 39
social workers, 61–62
Sudan, 41, 44

T

Tanzania, 56
tetanus, 28, 30
Tostan, 53

U

Uganda, 72
United Kingdom (UK), 8, 59
  fight against FGC in the UK, 40,
    49, 62, 63
United Nations, 47, 56, 58
United Nations Children's Fund
    (UNICEF), 11, 43, 44, 46, 50,
    53, 56, 59
United Nations Population Fund
    (UNFPA), 43, 48
U.S. Department of State, 48, 68
uterus, 18, 23, 31

V

"vacation cutting," 40, 59, 61, 68
vagina, 22–24, 25, 29, 31, 32, 35

Valverde, Donna, 72–73, 74
Valvisions Foundation, 72–73
  victims of FGC
  support and resources for, 10, 49,
    58–74
  who is at risk, 10, 11, 19–20, 48,
    57, 60–63
vulva, 24, 28

W

Walker, Alice, 54–55
women, control of, 14–19
World Health Organization (WHO),
    10, 14, 15, 19, 22, 25, 31, 32,
    43, 45, 47, 51–52, 59

Y

Yousafzai, Malala, 65

About the Author

Writer and educator Terry Teague Meyer lives in Houston, Texas. She has lived in France and traveled extensively, including to Africa. She has written several books on social issues and works for social change by volunteering as a mentor and teacher of English as a second language within immigrant communities.

Photo Credits

Cover © iStockphoto.com/AveryPhotography; pp. 8-9, 29, 39, 47, 50, 59 © AP Images; p. 12 © Nucleus Medical Art, Inc/Phototake; pp. 13, 26-27 Gwen Shockey/Science Source; p. 16 Print Collector/ Hulton Archive/Getty Images; p. 17 Palazzo Ducale, Venice, Italy/ Bridgeman Images; p. 19 Johnuniq/Wikimedia Commons/File: FGM prevalence UNICEF 2013.svg/CC BY-SA 4.0; p. 23 Encyclopaedia Britannica/UIG/Getty Images; p. 32 Reuters/Landov; p. 35 Dai Kurokawa/EPA/Landov; p. 36 Adek Berry/AFP/Getty Images; p. 40 Justin Tallis/AFP/Getty Images; p. 41 Cris Bouroncle/AFP/ Getty Images; p. 45 Finbarr O'Reilly/Reuters/Landov; p. 46 Jemal Countess/Getty Images; p. 52 Ben Hider/Getty Images; p. 55 Monica Morgan/WireImage/Getty Images; p. 60 forma.fgc.org. Used with permission. Photo by Nicole DiMella; p. 64 © ZUMA Press, Inc./ Alamy; p. 71 BSIP/Universal Images Group/Getty Images; p. 75 © 2005 Netsanet Assaye, Courtesy of PhotoshareDesigner: Nicole Russo; Editor: Kathy Kuhtz Campbell